3/10/11

You know it's love when you share your cupcake.
—The Cupcake Chef

ISABELLA ANJULI

A Cupcake Affair.
Tempt, Tease and Bake Your Way to the Top

Asher Drake Publishing Inc.
P.O. Box 1113, Walled Lake, MI 48390

The information in this book and the accompanying websites are intended to provide helpful and informative materials on the subject addressed. It is not intended as a substitute for professional medical advice. You should consult a health care professional in regards to your specific situation.

Library of Congress Cataloging-in-Publication Data

Anjuli, Isabella.
   A cupcake affair: tempt, tease and bake your way to the top/
   Isabella Anjuli—Special Edition   p.   cm.
Includes bibliographical references and index.
Library of Congress Control Number: 2010909003
ISBN-10: 0-9845774-0-8
ISBN-13: 978-0-9845774-0-8
1. Cupcakes   2. Baking   I. Title

Editor: Donna Schwontkowski
Book Design by Jana Rade, Impact Studios
Cover Design by Rosie Grupp, Book Studio
Cover Photography by Ruth Black, United Kingdom

# Dedication

To my best friend Roya,
who lives on with every beat of my heart.

My two beautiful daughters,
who I know will always do good things.

To Kevin, for all the wonderful memories,
and for always being there.

And

to all the cupcakes over the years
whose lives were cruelly & prematurely ended
before they ever started
so this book could be born

and so the lives of billions of future cupcakes could be saved.

*"Eating is not merely a material pleasure. Eating well gives a spectacular joy to life and contributes immensely to goodwill and happy companionship. It is of great importance to the morale."*

Elsa Schiaparelli, Italian designer (1890-1973)

# Table Of Contents

Dedication . . . . . . . . . . . . . . . . . . . . . . . . . . . . . . . . . . 11

Acknowledgements . . . . . . . . . . . . . . . . . . . . . . . . . . . 23

The Secret Reasons Behind this Book . . . . . . . . . . . . . . . . 25

How to Use this Book . . . . . . . . . . . . . . . . . . . . . . . . . . 29

PART 1 UNFORGETTABLE CUPCAKE BASICS

Chapter 1:   The Unforgettable Cupcake Love Affair  . . . . . .  33

The Evolution of the Cupcake . . . . . . . . . . . . . . . . . . . 34

The Outlaw Cupcake . . . . . . . . . . . . . . . . . . . . . . . . . 35

Chapter 2:   Cupcake Fame, Fun and Fortune . . . . . . . . . . .  37

How to Make Someone Feel
   Very Special with Cupcakes . . . . . . . . . . . . . . . . . . 37

How to Be More Romantic Using Cupcakes . . . . . . . . . . 39

How to Use Cupcakes to Close Business Deals, Sell
   More Products, and Generate Customer Loyalty . . . . 42

Checklist for Your Local Cupcake Bakery to Buy
   or Design the Perfect Cupcakes . . . . . . . . . . . . . . . 45

Cupcake Statistics. . . . . . . . . . . . . . . . . . . . . . . . . . . 47

Chapter 3:   The Secrets behind Light, Fluffy Cupcakes . . . .  51

How to Ensure Light, Fluffy Cupcakes  . . . . . . . . . . . . . 52

The Closely Guarded Secret of Cupcakeaholics  . . . . . . 53

Homemade Mixes . . . . . . . . . . . . . . . . . . . . . . . . . . . 54

Box Mixes . . . . . . . . . . . . . . . . . . . . . . . . . . . . . . . . 55

How Professional Pastry Chefs Create Unforgettable
    Cupcakes: Their Secret Ritual . . . . . . . . . . . . . . . . . . . 59
Chapter 4:  The Distance Between Disappointment
  and Divine  . . . . . . . . . . . . . . . . . . . . . . . . . . . . . . . . . 61
    Pre-Baking Rituals (before you crack a single egg)  . . . . 63
    Ratios Determine Your Results . . . . . . . . . . . . . . . . . . . 64
    The Perfect Oven Temperature . . . . . . . . . . . . . . . . . . . 65
    Selecting the Perfect Cupcake Tin  . . . . . . . . . . . . . . . 65
    How to Ensure Easy Cupcake Removal . . . . . . . . . . . . . 67

PART 2 THE BEST CUPCAKE INGREDIENTS

Chapter 5:  Introduction to Cupcake Ingredients . . . . . . . . 73
Chapter 6:  Flours  . . . . . . . . . . . . . . . . . . . . . . . . . . . . . . 75
    Testing Flour You Have Stored for Freshness  . . . . . . . 75
    Shopping for Fresh Flour . . . . . . . . . . . . . . . . . . . . . . . 75
    How to Store Flour to Extend Freshness . . . . . . . . . . . 77
    Finding Just the Right Cupcake Flour . . . . . . . . . . . . . 78
    The Heartbreak that Hides in the Flour . . . . . . . . . . . 81
    When to Sift the Flour  . . . . . . . . . . . . . . . . . . . . . . . 82
    Flours Not Made for Unforgettable Cupcakes  . . . . . . . 82
    Protein Percentages in Flour. . . . . . . . . . . . . . . . . . . . . 83
    How Gluten-Free, Vegan and Healthier Cupcakes Can
      Taste Unforgettable (in a blissful way). . . . . . . . . . . . 84
    Health Benefits of Non-Gluten Flours . . . . . . . . . . . . . 86
Chapter 7:  The Magic of Emulsifiers in Cupcakes  . . . . . . . 89
Chapter 8:  Leavening Your Cupcakes . . . . . . . . . . . . . . . . . 91
    Baking Soda in Cupcake Recipes . . . . . . . . . . . . . . . . . 91
    Is Baking Powder Better than Baking Soda? . . . . . . . . . 92
    How to Test Your Chemical Leaveners for Freshness . . . 93

Chapter 9: The Role of Butter, Shortenings and Oils in
Creating Unforgettable Cupcakes . . . . . . . . . . . . . . . . . . . . 95
    Fat (Butter and Oil Substitution) Chart. . . . . . . . . . . . . 98
    Butter Volume & Weight Equivalents . . . . . . . . . . . . . . 101
    How to Test Fats for Freshness . . . . . . . . . . . . . . . . . . . 102
    Healthy Oil Substitutions (and Reducing Fat) . . . . . . . 102
Chapter 10: Sugar Does More than Sweeten Cupcakes . . . . 105
    Sugar Substitutes . . . . . . . . . . . . . . . . . . . . . . . . . . . . . . 106
    Agave as a Sweetener . . . . . . . . . . . . . . . . . . . . . . . . . . 107
    Stevia as a Sweetener . . . . . . . . . . . . . . . . . . . . . . . . . . . 107
    Xylitol as a Sugar Substitute . . . . . . . . . . . . . . . . . . . . 110
    Sugar Substitution Chart . . . . . . . . . . . . . . . . . . . . . . . 112

Chapter 11: Eggs . . . . . . . . . . . . . . . . . . . . . . . . . . . . . . . . . . 115
    How to Test Your Eggs for Freshness . . . . . . . . . . . . . . 116
    How to Separate Eggs . . . . . . . . . . . . . . . . . . . . . . . . . . 117
    Egg Whites in Cupcake Recipes . . . . . . . . . . . . . . . . . . 118
    Whole Eggs in Cupcake Recipes . . . . . . . . . . . . . . . . . . 118
    Egg Substitution Chart . . . . . . . . . . . . . . . . . . . . . . . . . 119
    Eggs as a Partial Sugar Substitute . . . . . . . . . . . . . . . . 121
Chapter 12: Cupcake Mix-Ins . . . . . . . . . . . . . . . . . . . . . . . . 123
Chapter 13: What Ingredients Do
in Your Cupcake Recipes . . . . . . . . . . . . . . . . . . . . . . . . . . 125
    By Function . . . . . . . . . . . . . . . . . . . . . . . . . . . . . . . . . . 126
    By Ingredient . . . . . . . . . . . . . . . . . . . . . . . . . . . . . . . . 127
Chapter 14: The Right Temperature for Ingredients . . . . . 131
    No Time? How to Warm Ingredients to Room
        Temperature . . . . . . . . . . . . . . . . . . . . . . . . . . . . . 132
    How to Warm Eggs . . . . . . . . . . . . . . . . . . . . . . . . . . . 132
    How to Warm Butter . . . . . . . . . . . . . . . . . . . . . . . . . . 132
    How to Warm Milk or Other Liquids . . . . . . . . . . . . . 133

# PART 3 THE PERFECT BATTER

Chapter 15: Preparing the Batter for
Unforgettable Cupcakes .......................... 137
    Methods of Mixing for Unforgettable Cupcakes ..... 137
    General Guidelines for Mixing Cupcake Batter ...... 138
Chapter 16: How to Choose the Mixing Method
for Cupcake Recipes ............................ 141
    The Muffin Method .......................... 142
    The Creaming Method ........................ 144
    The Rubbing in Method ...................... 145
    The Egg Foam Method ....................... 146
    The Melted Method .......................... 147
    Other Methods.............................. 148

# PART 4 TO LINE OR NOT TO LINE: FILLING THE WELLS

Chapter 17: Introducing Cupcake Liners ............... 153
    The Sweet ................................. 153
    The Sour .................................. 154
    The Solution to Cupcake Liner Problems ........... 155
Chapter 18: Solving Cupcake Liner Problems........... 157
    Cupcake Liner Separation Issue Solution ........... 157
    Cupcake Liner Sticking Issue Solution ............. 158
Chapter 19: Filling the Cupcake Wells ................. 161

# PART 5 BAKING: RISE UP AND COOL DOWN WITHOUT THE COLLAPSE

Chapter 20: Secrets to the Baking Phase . . . . . . . . . . . . . . . 167

Cupcake Cool Down . . . . . . . . . . . . . . . . . . . . . . . . . . 169

# PART 6 FROSTINGS, GLAZES AND ICINGS

Chapter 21: All About Buttercreams, Whipped Cream

Frostings, and Cream Frostings . . . . . . . . . . . . . . . . . . . 175

Eggs in Frosting . . . . . . . . . . . . . . . . . . . . . . . . . . . . 175

Pairing the Cupcake with the Frosting . . . . . . . . . . . . . 176

Buttercreams . . . . . . . . . . . . . . . . . . . . . . . . . . . . . 176

Italian Buttercream . . . . . . . . . . . . . . . . . . . . . . . . . 177

Swiss Buttercream . . . . . . . . . . . . . . . . . . . . . . . . . . 177

French Buttercream . . . . . . . . . . . . . . . . . . . . . . . . . 177

Simple Buttercream . . . . . . . . . . . . . . . . . . . . . . . . . 177

Golden Buttercream . . . . . . . . . . . . . . . . . . . . . . . . . 177

Whipped Cream Frostings. . . . . . . . . . . . . . . . . . . . . 178

Cream Frostings. . . . . . . . . . . . . . . . . . . . . . . . . . . . 178

Egg-White Frostings. . . . . . . . . . . . . . . . . . . . . . . . . 179

Seven-Minute Frosting. . . . . . . . . . . . . . . . . . . . . . . . 180

Boiled or Fluffy Frosting . . . . . . . . . . . . . . . . . . . . . . 180

Chapter 22: Chocolate Frostings . . . . . . . . . . . . . . . . . . 181

Fudge . . . . . . . . . . . . . . . . . . . . . . . . . . . . . . . . . . 181

Chocolate Buttercream . . . . . . . . . . . . . . . . . . . . . . . 181

Simple Chocolate Buttercream . . . . . . . . . . . . . . . . . . 181

White Chocolate Cream . . . . . . . . . . . . . . . . . . . . . . 181

Ganache . . . . . . . . . . . . . . . . . . . . . . . . . . . . . . . . 182

Traditional Ganache . . . . . . . . . . . . . . . . . . . . . . . . . 182

Truffled Ganache . . . . . . . . . . . . . . . . . . . . . . . . . . . 182

Milk Chocolate Truffle . . . . . . . . . . . . . . . . . . . . . 182
White Truffle . . . . . . . . . . . . . . . . . . . . . . . . . . . . 182
Satin Ganache . . . . . . . . . . . . . . . . . . . . . . . . . . . 182
Chapter 23: Glazes and Icings . . . . . . . . . . . . . . . . . . 185
Decorative Icings . . . . . . . . . . . . . . . . . . . . . . . . . 185
Decorator's Buttercream . . . . . . . . . . . . . . . . . 186
Fondant . . . . . . . . . . . . . . . . . . . . . . . . . . . . . . . 186
Royal Icing . . . . . . . . . . . . . . . . . . . . . . . . . . . . . 186
Specialty Frostings . . . . . . . . . . . . . . . . . . . . . . . 186
Non-Fat/Low-Fat . . . . . . . . . . . . . . . . . . . . . . . . 186
Dulce de Leche . . . . . . . . . . . . . . . . . . . . . . . . . 187
Agave-Based Frostings . . . . . . . . . . . . . . . . . . . . 187
Yogurt-Based Frostings . . . . . . . . . . . . . . . . . . . 187
Fruit . . . . . . . . . . . . . . . . . . . . . . . . . . . . . . . . . . 187
Dairy-Free . . . . . . . . . . . . . . . . . . . . . . . . . . . . . 187
Frosting and Icing Chart . . . . . . . . . . . . . . . . . . . 188

PART 7 ADVANCED CUPCAKING

Chapter 24: Create Your Own Cupcake Recipes
from Scratch . . . . . . . . . . . . . . . . . . . . . . . . . . . . 193
The Flour/Sugar Ratio . . . . . . . . . . . . . . . . . . . . 194
The Eggs/Butter Ratio . . . . . . . . . . . . . . . . . . . . 194
The Eggs and Liquid to Sugar Ratio . . . . . . . . . . 195
Chemical Leavening . . . . . . . . . . . . . . . . . . . . . . 195
Flavor Enhancing . . . . . . . . . . . . . . . . . . . . . . . . 195
Chapter 25: How to Create Filled and
Stuffed Cupcakes Like a Pro . . . . . . . . . . . . . . . . . 197
The Difference Between Filling and Stuffing . . . . . . 198
Professional Tips to Filling Cupcakes . . . . . . . . . . 198
The Basics About Fillings . . . . . . . . . . . . . . . . . . 198

Creamy Fillings . . . . . . . . . . . . . . . . . . . . . . . . . 199

Fruit Fillings . . . . . . . . . . . . . . . . . . . . . . . . . . . 199

Heavy Fillings . . . . . . . . . . . . . . . . . . . . . . . . . . 200

Chapter 26: Professional Cupcake Filling and

Stuffing Methods . . . . . . . . . . . . . . . . . . . . . . . . 201

Insertion Method . . . . . . . . . . . . . . . . . . . . . . . . . 201

Removal Method . . . . . . . . . . . . . . . . . . . . . . . . . 202

Layering Method . . . . . . . . . . . . . . . . . . . . . . . . . 203

Partially-Baked Method . . . . . . . . . . . . . . . . . . . . . 205

Self-Filling Method. . . . . . . . . . . . . . . . . . . . . . . . 205

Bonus Recipe for High End Filling . . . . . . . . . . . . . 206

Ice Cream Filled Cupcakes . . . . . . . . . . . . . . . . . . 207

Stuffed Cupcakes . . . . . . . . . . . . . . . . . . . . . . . . 207

Ten Ideas for Stuffing Cupcakes . . . . . . . . . . . . . . . 208

## PART 8 HOW TO STORE, TRANSPORT AND SHIP CUPCAKES

Chapter 27: Storing and Freezing Cupcakes . . . . . . . . . . . . 213

Storing Cupcakes . . . . . . . . . . . . . . . . . . . . . . . . 214

Freezing Cupcakes . . . . . . . . . . . . . . . . . . . . . . . 214

Individually Wrapping Cupcakes . . . . . . . . . . . . . . . 215

Wrapping an Unfrosted Cupcake . . . . . . . . . . . . . . . 216

Wrapping a Frosted Cupcake . . . . . . . . . . . . . . . . . 216

Cupcake Carrying Cases . . . . . . . . . . . . . . . . . . . . 217

Chapter 28: Homemade and Reusable Cupcake Shipping

Containers . . . . . . . . . . . . . . . . . . . . . . . . . . . . 219

Packaging Cupcakes for a Car Ride . . . . . . . . . . . . . 220

Packing Cupcakes for Shipping . . . . . . . . . . . . . . . . 220

Traveling Cupcakes . . . . . . . . . . . . . . . . . . . . . . . 221

Displaying Cupcakes . . . . . . . . . . . . . . . . . . . . . . 224

# PART 9 MASTERING THE ART OF UNFORGETTABLE CUPCAKES

Chapter 29: Frequently Asked Questions
& Troubleshooting ............................... 229

# PART 10  RECIPES

Basic Vanilla Cupcake Recipe ..................... 263
Basic Gluten-Free Vanilla Cupcake Recipe .......... 265
Simple Buttercream Frosting ..................... 269
Flavored Versions of Simple Buttercream Frosting ... 269
Chocolate Mascarpone Filling .................... 270
Brown Sugar Buttercream   (an Italian Buttercream) . 271

# PART 11 APPENDICES

Appendix A: Recipe Conversions ...................... 277
Converting to U.S. from Metric ................... 277
Converting to Metric from U.S. ................... 277
Volume Measures Conversions ..................... 278
Volume Measurement Equivalents ................. 279
Key Fahrenheit To Celsius Equivalents.............. 280
Adjusting Cupcake Recipes for Humidity .......... 281
Adjusting Cupcake Recipes for Altitude............. 282

Appendix B: Substitutions .......................... 285
Miscellaneous Ingredient Substitutions ............ 285
Flour & Flour Substitutes–Weight, Measurement and
Nutrition Equivalents ......................... 294
Appendix C: Cupcake Baking Terminology ............. 299

Appendix D: Checklists . . . . . . . . . . . . . . . . . . . . . . . . . . . . 307
   Cupcake Baking Checklist . . . . . . . . . . . . . . . . . . . . . . 307
   Cupcake Ingredient Tips to Ensure Unforgettable
     Cupcakes . . . . . . . . . . . . . . . . . . . . . . . . . . . . . . . . 309
Appendix E: Calculating the Calories and
  Weight Watcher® Points for Your Cupcakes . . . . . . . . . . . 311
Appendix F: Readings and Resources . . . . . . . . . . . . . . . . . 317
Appendix G: Online Tools . . . . . . . . . . . . . . . . . . . . . . . . . 327
   Great Cupcake Blogs . . . . . . . . . . . . . . . . . . . . . . . . . . 327
   Other Sweet Blogs . . . . . . . . . . . . . . . . . . . . . . . . . . . . 328
   About the Author. . . . . . . . . . . . . . . . . . . . . . . . . . . . . 339
   About the Publisher. . . . . . . . . . . . . . . . . . . . . . . . . . . 341

# Acknowledgements

No book is written in a vacuum; an author has so many people to thank that it would take a lifetime. However, there are several that should be noted here. Nothing is ever possible without Mom. My mom gave me a love of baking through our many Christmas baking rituals. She gave me a love that has allowed me to focus on the small seemingly insignificant details of life that contain most of the sweetness. Thank you, MOM!

Thank you to all the divine masters who have inspired and guided me through all my adventures in baking: Julia Child, the Goddess of Culinary Mastery; Graham Kerr, "The Galloping Gourmet"; Martha Stewart, the Domestic Superwoman; Paula Deen, the warm and wonderful soulful kitchen magician; Emerill Lagasse, the master of flavor perfection; Rachel Ray, the inventor of the easy button in the kitchen; Alton Brown, my favorite food detective; Nigella Lawson, for her inspiring and unabashed worship of food; Ree Drummond, for her mouth-watering recipes and constant inspiration; Stephanie Bailey for her contributions to the research and writing of parts of the book including some of her own recipes, Ann Convery (Genius), for her guidance and priceless input, and all my cupcake Twitter friends who give me an endless source of inspiration and cupcake ideas through their blog posts and insights.

Thank you also to Michael Buble and Harry Connick, Jr., for the perfect soundtracks to use while practicing unforgettable and taste bud enchanting cupcake art.

# The Secret Reasons Behind This Book: a.k.a. "How to Tempt, Tease and Enchant Taste Buds Around the World"

This book is a collection of helpful cupcake information, facts, tips, secrets, friends' secrets and 'Ah ha's' I have accumulated in my more than 35 years of baking.

Once I began assembling the book, I realized I did not know when to stop. I also realized there are a lot of questions out there about cupcakes that have never been answered nor assembled in one place.

There is so much information here about making cupcakes that you will have new appreciation for the masterpiece that a delicious cupcake is, and the absolute genius your local cupcake bakery is as their bakers create those lovely little personal cakes that fit in the cup of your hand. You will also realize how time and labor intensive a memorable cupcake is.

According to a New York Times November 2009 article, you are not alone if you share the new entrepreneurial dream of selling cupcakes. Even better, cupcake sales are projected to rise 20% over the next 5 years, exceeding the sales of all other baked goods that are projected to rise only in the single digits. Statistics say when a new cupcake shop opens, sales grow for the other cupcake shops in the area.

You may want to become the next cupcake sensation in your neighborhood or on the Internet. You may want to learn how to make your cupcakes healthier, grow your appreciation for the perfect cupcakes that your favorite bakery makes, or create special memories for your children. Whatever taste bud temptation you have in mind, *A Cupcake Affair* will guide you on the unforgettable, taste bud enchanting journey.

# How to Use this Book

This book is written for you to use in many ways. You can go to a section and read that section; you can access the charts for substituting ingredients, or read the FAQ section which answers the most frequently asked questions about making cupcakes. You can also reference the reading and resources section, find a particular subject from the index, scan the notes called out throughout the book, and, of course, you can read it from front to back cover. Whatever way you read or reference your cupcake making affairs, be sure to:

- **Join the Happy Cupcake Community at www.CupcakeAffair.com** and find new cupcake friends, get checklists, member only cupcake recipes, cupcake science experiment results, free stuff, tips and much more.
- Follow the Cupcake Chef on **Twitter@CupcakeChef**
- Visit the **Cupcake Inspiration Index on www.CupcakeDecoratingU.com,** the inspiration for decorating your unforgettable cupcakes.
- If you have a question not answered in the book, find a typo, or have a suggestion please email me at **CupcakeChef@CupcakeAffair.com.**
- Get **taste bud enchanting headline grabbing news** at www.CupcakeAffair.com/breakingnews.

# Part 1

# Unforgettable Cupcake *Basics*

*Chapter 1*

# The Unforgettable Cupcake Love Affair

Cupcakes are poems written in sugar and flour. Masterpieces in confection. Heaven manifested in the cup of your hand. Scented clouds of sweet delights. Beautiful. Perfect. Unique. Crave-able. Whatever the season, cupcakes never go out of style. Popular for nearly two centuries, the cupcake ideal is often light, velvety, and fluffy. Soft and golden brown, never overdone. Cupcakes inspire like every great love affair.

Even if you have never in your life made a cupcake, from this day forth…you will know what it feels like to hold the power of creating heavenly perfection in your own kitchen.

**A Cupcake Affair** is the ultimate companion guide to the world of cupcake and cupcake recipes; a blueprint to the power of cupcake romance to tempt, tease and enslave taste buds.

Cupcakes are poems written in sugar and flour. Masterpieces in confection. Heaven manifested in the cup of your hand.

Even if you have never in your life made a cupcake, from this day forth…you will know what it feels like to hold the power of creating heavenly perfection in your own kitchen.

Cupcakes became popular because they had a shorter cooking time than traditional cakes.

Statistics say if a cupcake bakery opens in town it will increase sales at all other cupcake bakeries in town.

# The Evolution of the Cupcake

Cupcakes were accidentally invented in the 19th century when a baker poured his leftover cake batter into little cups and baked them. Cupcakes became popular because they had a shorter cooking time than traditional cakes. It was simple to remember the ingredients: one spoonful of baking soda, one cup of milk, one cup of butter, two cups of sugar, three cups of flour, and four eggs. In the early 20th century, when cupcake tins were invented, baking cupcakes became even simpler.

The introduction of Betty Crocker's easy cake mixes in the late 1940s made baking the tiny cakes quicker and easier than ever, and cupcakes became synonymous with homemaking in the 1950s. Cupcake ingredients and toppings have changed a lot over time, but the popularity of the tiny dessert has only grown. They are popular treats for birthday parties, social events and school functions. Cupcakes fit in anywhere: at the family picnic, the potluck dinner and even Fifth Avenue weddings.

Cupcake bakeries thrive in cities across the country, offering the traditional chocolate and vanilla flavors, and modern variations like bacon, peanut butter, and mint chocolate chip. Cupcakes, chic and modern, are an ideal American comfort food. Countless blogs, websites and books are devoted to them. Statistics say if a cupcake bakery opens in town it will increase sales at all other cupcake bakeries. It's the same with love. The more you love, the more love there is. Coincidence? I think not!

## The Outlaw Cupcake

A cupcake ban in Texas caused such a riot that the "Safe Cupcake" Amendment was passed and added to the Texas state nutrition policy.

When a school district in Alexandria, Virginia, banned cupcakes from their classrooms in 2006 as part of their wellness program, parents were outraged. Many other states, including New York, Pennsylvania, and California, have since joined the anti-cupcake movement and imposed similar bans in an effort to stop childhood obesity. A cupcake ban in Texas caused such a riot that the "Safe Cupcake" Amendment was passed and added to the Texas state nutrition policy. The Safe Cupcake Amendment assures parents' right to bring cupcakes for school celebrations such as birthdays and Halloween.

No matter what they are for, cupcakes brighten any occasion. There are thousands of recipes out there, all claiming to create the best cup-sized confection. Yet, some of them are so dry or tasteless that not even the frothiest

By following the guidelines and recommendations in "A Cupcake Affair" you will discover how to create a batch of cupcakes that will make you the most in-demand, popular guest at every social function.

You are about to discover everything you need to know to make cupcakes that will make You unforgettable.

icing can save them. Even a good recipe must be followed <u>exactly</u> in order to create light, fluffy and golden brown desserts.

The right ingredients are important. Preparing the kitchen and readying the supplies makes for easier and more successful cupcake baking. Mixing the ingredients to perfection creates light, fluffy and unforgettable cupcakes. By following the guidelines and recommendations in "A Cupcake Affair," you will discover how to create a batch of cupcakes that will make you the most in-demand, popular guest at every social function. Your friends and family will be begging you to reveal your secrets.

You are about to discover everything you need to know about how to make cupcakes that will make You unforgettable.

*Chapter 2*

# Cupcake Fame, Fun and Fortune

Cupcakes contain elements of the magical. Nowhere on Earth is there another food that has the same spellbinding qualities. No other food can mesmerize children and adults. The reason? Not only are the cupcakes themselves tied into our threads of memory, but so are the excitement, anticipation and pleasure. This puts the cupcake in the enviable position of being the one food that can make someone feel special when she is presented with a cupcake.

## How to Make Someone Feel Very Special with Cupcakes

Flowers, note cards, and custom MP3 mixes are a thing of the past. If you want to make someone feel loved and special, give them a box of cupcakes.

These sweet little islands of confectionery love are on the top of the food trends for good reason – they make any day a better day. With so many flavors to choose from and a wide array of colors and shapes for your eyes to gorge on, cupcakes are crowd pleasers, even in a crowd of one.

Cupcakes make people feel warm and fuzzy inside. Personal serving-sized, they coax a smile from the lips right from the start because they scream: "You don't have to share!" Add in the connection to sweet childhood memories of Mom's love and you have the trifecta of surrender.

It's true, in a recent survey conducted by Asher Drake Publishing, 97% of those people interviewed admitted that they would say "yes" to almost any question after eating a cupcake. Cupcakes have the power to bond people together just like other good food and conversation, but cupcakes say it with sweetness and nostalgia. Sharing food helps develop a bond between people and paves the road to more good times. Cupcakes are like the superglue of food bonding.

To guys out there struggling to find a romantic idea, why not give your girlfriend a cupcake and creatively spell out your feelings to her using the cupcake's designs? Surprise her at work. How about sending her a specially wrapped cupcake?

If you are on a team and you've just won a game, treat your teammates to a cupcake trophy. If you are a mom and your son just handed you his report card with flying colors, give him a cupcake treat that he will remember forever. You can give a whole box of cupcakes to your mom thanking her for giving birth to you. Or give a single cupcake to a friend after a disagreement.

Even without a special occasion, treating your friends and family to a boxful of yummy cupcakes any day will become a memory imprinted in their minds for a long time. No matter what the celebration is, or who you are planning to give them to, cupcakes pave the way into hearts everywhere.

## How to Be More Romantic Using Cupcakes

Everyone knows about Cupid fluttering around, propelled by little wings, armed with a bow and arrow. Cupid sets his sights and takes aim randomly. In Roman mythology, if a person is hit with Cupid's arrows, that person's fate is to fall deeply in love.

If this were true, perhaps millions of men, seeking their dream girls' affection, would line up to ask this Roman god for real help.

Although considered a myth, gently prodding someone to fall in love with you isn't that hard to do.

Peter Sozou and Robert  Seymour's research help us answer the following question: "What is the way to a woman's heart?" Their study revealed that men who take women out on dates rather than shower them with expensive gifts end up in happier, genuine relationships.

It turns out that women love to be loved and cherished through sincere acts rather than through being showered with meaningless gifts. And how to show you are sincere?

The answer is simple – cupcakes.

Go ahead, laugh and ignore the fact, but cupcakes actually work like Cupid's bow and arrow… except that it is not a good idea to aim and fire cupcakes at your crush.

Tap into your romantic side and reach out to the local cupcake bakery for help in choosing the perfect cupcake wrapped for a special occasion.

Here is an idea to ramp up the romance.

- Stir things up with a fresh angle. Give her a bouquet of cupcakes instead of flowers.

Want to pump it up to the next level? Bake the cupcakes yourself and customize them to her liking. If she loves chocolate then boost up that cupcake with chocolate flavored batter and add some chocolate chips. Top it off with a swirl of white chocolate Ganache. A perfect, romantic declaration.

Here are some additional ideas to help you declare your affection:

- Write a message on a cupcake. Spell out your feelings through fondant letters on a cupcake.
- Not great at baking cupcakes? Seek help from your local bakery. Get yourself plain, undecorated cupcakes with classic delicious flavors. Whip up some edible fondant letters and form words as you arrange your cupcakes in a box. Her heart will melt with joy.
- Don't want to fuss at all? Contact your local bakery to discuss whipping up a special cupcake or batch of cupcakes just for your sweetie, all inclusive. Cupcake, frosting, and special presentation.
- How about a cupcake treasure hunt? Hide cupcakes around the house or get your friends to

help out in a town-wide hunt and add a clue on top of each cupcake with a hint of where to locate the next one. At the end, how about a cupcake along with tickets to a hot, upcoming event?

- Add something special. Proposing to the woman of your dreams? Place the diamond ring on top of the cupcake. Please don't place anything inedible inside the cupcake as small things can be a choking hazard.

The advantages of cupcakes over other gifts for a love interest?

- Cupcakes are inexpensive. The cost of baking cupcakes is only the cost of the ingredients or the cost of a couple of cupcakes at the local bakery.
- Spend quality time with her. A date to the movies doesn't help you get to know her better. You spend your time staring at the screen rather than talking to each other. Baking cupcakes together or sharing yourself over cupcakes and coffee from the local bakery opens the conversation to memories and the talk of family.
- Discover the joy of baking cupcakes and the joy returned to you when you present them.
- It's a great chance to show off and impress with a thoughtful gift that says, "You are important to me."

Cupcakes simply make everyone happy. Plus, if you purchase cupcakes from a local bakery and get a few different kinds, you can share your cupcake. Since cupcakes are single servings already, by sharing a cupcake you signal to the other person you are giving and trusting. And it paves a shortcut to her heart.

Cupcakes can also pave the way to other successes...

## How to Use Cupcakes to Close Business Deals, Sell More Products, and Generate Customer Loyalty

In the world of commerce, cupcakes are king. It's well known in marketing circles that great food is the highway to good feelings about your company, brand, and sale. Providing great food to customers has increased sales up to 34% or more.

Though well known, it is not so well practiced. Somewhere in the translation, "great food" becomes stale cookies and coffee reminiscent of oil balls collected from the Gulf Coast, steeped in water. Businesses are looking for a cheap path to increased sales. The point missed? The food you serve is the message you send to your customers about you and the value you place on them as customers. Serve cheap food, attract cheap customers, and you insult your business and potential clients in the process. Lost in the translation between "great food" and stale cookies? It's all about trust when it comes to sales. Serve the wrong food and you could actually hurt your sales.

Cupcakes are the inexpensive yet luxurious treat that announces your business and your clients are important. Cupcakes are an exciting treat that can be dressed up for any occasion. Who else can cupcakes impress in the course of a business day? Co-workers, partners, suppliers, service personnel, the UPS delivery person, the mail carrier, the teller at the bank. With a smart-looking suit to impress and a cupcake in hand, who knows what doors could open from this simple gesture of kindness?

Business event? Forget the boring bagels. Bring a box of cupcakes!

Where else could you use cupcakes? Desperately trying to close a business deal? Bring a box of cupcakes to your business meeting. Remember that fact about 97% of people reporting they were likely to say "yes" to any question after eating a cupcake? Uh huh, that's right, this applies to business questions, too.

Perhaps you are wondering why this is so. Is there something about cupcakes that seems to be so good that they will trigger a change in the way a person thinks?

In a book entitled, "You're Working Too Hard to Make the Sale!", William Books and Thomas Travisano researched how a buyer's emotional triggers influence the sales outcome from the very first business meeting. The conclusion was that buyers and potential clients give in to the salesperson that seems to be open and welcome to fulfilling their wants first rather than their needs.

Bring in a bunch of cupcakes and your client will remember you for providing an indulgence they didn't realize they craved. Tie a first impression to the one food that opens mouths, hearts, and minds. Happy prospects, clients who are wowed, and customers who feel important tie positive feelings to a person who comes bearing cupcakes.

People who own businesses can also offer cupcakes as an incentive. A little known fact about purchases is that people buy on emotion. That is, emotion about a small detail about what they are considering to buy. People buy a house because it has a single beautiful library. They buy an educational course because it includes a particular topic in detail, and so on. Can someone sell something if a dozen cupcakes are a bonus? Yes, the same reason people open checking accounts to get toasters, except that cupcakes are a more enticing and more immediate reward. People begin to salivate just at the sight of cupcakes. Evil? No, not if your product fulfills its need. You will not serve cupcakes to sell a product or service that you wouldn't sell your grandmother… Try this and watch it backfire. Not even a cupcake can prevent karma's visit.

More ideas for cupcakes in the business setting:

- Give away a cupcake or two for every person who:
    - Spends $25 (one cupcake for every $25 spent)
    - Books an appointment
    - Visits an open house
    - Has an investment review

- Gets his taxes done
- Pays for carpet cleaning
- Brings his car in for an oil change

If a customer knows he is in for a sweet treat when he visits a business, don't you think that business will build a loyal following, fast? Oh, yes.

Here's a tip: Put in a recurring order at your local bakery for a dozen of their best cupcakes. Think about all the business you can bring in. A small investment in cupcakes can be responsible for closing a six-figure deal.

## Checklist for Your Local Cupcake Bakery to Buy or Design the Perfect Cupcakes

Here are a few tips and a critical checklist to ensure your local bakery has everything it needs to create cupcakes that will pave the way for destiny to take a hand.

- Know your customers. Before going ahead to the bakery or cupcake shop of your choice, consider the customers before ordering a cupcake. For example, you can make a list of your customers' traits.
  - Savvy and sophisticated or practical and down to earth?
  - Men, women, or a mix?
  - What kind of foods do your potential clients typically dine on?
  - Do they have discriminating palates? You do not want to serve really sweet cupcakes to

someone with a discriminating palate. You will need a sophisticated flavor that doesn't rely on sugar for flavor.

- Health conscious prospects? Healthier choices exist and your local bakery may already have a tasty selection of organic, gluten free, and low-fat choices.
- Are colors or particular flavors important to include or avoid?
- Allergy sensitive clientele? Allergy free choices are a must. Ask your local bakeries what choices they can provide. Gluten, nut, dairy, and egg allergies can all be accommodated in a cupcake recipe. You could offer to pay a local bakery to develop that one specific cupcake for you if you will be placing a weekly order.
- Search intently. If you're in a place where there is only one bakery that produces cupcakes, then you can search online. Online cupcake companies are exploding, and they deliver. You may find one that will even develop and decorate a cupcake with your client or prospective client's logo on it. If you are in a city with dozens of cupcake shops to choose from, then you need to search for the right cupcake bakery that caters to your needs and, at the same time, accommodates your desires. Do they deliver?
- Communicate and compromise (but not on flavor). Most cupcake bakeries already have a

brochure or even a website that shows off their products and packages. You have to talk to the store personnel, or better yet the baker or owner herself. Show your list and explain your needs. If you will be a regular customer of the bakery and you will be putting their name in front of other potential customers, they will work with you to get the cupcakes exactly right.

- Clarify and finalize. Once all things are set, double check to see if the bakery has the correct date and time for the delivery, and double check to ensure the order is correct. To limit the margin of error, make sure both parties understand all the details.

These are just a few tips and ideas, but they are probably the most important things to keep in mind when asking assistance from your local cupcake bakery. This is a win-win situation for the bakery and the business.

## Cupcake Statistics

Based on a survey of 694 people, here are some fun cupcake statistics: 95.3% of the total respondents love cupcakes. Overall, 94.9% of the females and 95.76% of the males are in love with cupcakes.

Here's the breakdown of cupcake lovers in percentage of different age groups:

| | |
|---|---|
| 18-22 | 96.7% |
| 23-27 | 94.3% |
| 28-32 | 92.5% |
| 33-37 | 98.8% |
| 38-42 | 92.3% |
| 43-47 | 92.3% |
| 48-52 | 95.5% |
| 53-57 | 95.5% |
| 58-71 | 100% |

Here are a few other interesting facts:
- As income increases over $50,000 per year, so does the percentage of people who like cupcakes, all the way up to 97.3%. When you reach $100,000 or more per year, the statistic dips to 87.4%.
- Only 21.43% live near a bakery
- 65.3% prefer to buy cupcakes
- 39.2% prefer to make cupcakes
- Chocolate frosting is preferred over vanilla frosting, 65.2% to 34.8%, which is 2 to 1 in favor of chocolate.
- The favorite kind of cupcake? Chocolate cupcakes made from melted chocolate.
- The favorite cupcake frosting combination?

Chocolate with chocolate frosting.
* The favorite chocolate cupcake? Chocolate with a molten chocolate center.

· · · · · · · · · · · · · · · · · · · · · · · · · · · · · · · · · · · · · · · · · · · · · · · · · · ·

*Chapter 3*

# The Secrets Behind Light, Fluffy Cupcakes

The goal of baking the cupcake is to get the batter to rise and trap the air bubbles created in the batter preparation phase in a tender, flavorful crumb before the heat from the top of the oven forms the crust on the cupcake and seals the tiny structure of bubbles in the batter.

Bubbles. Yep, bubbles are the secret behind spectacular cupcakes. Both the number of air bubbles and the amount of expansion you trigger by adding leavening agents are important. Air bubbles and leavening are critical elements in the chemistry behind creating light and fluffy cupcakes versus something you need to shellac and give away as a paper weight.

Bubbles are the secret behind spectacular cupcakes.

In order for the cupcakes to rise, a leavening agent must be mixed into the batter. The leavening agents used in most cupcake recipes are baking powder, baking soda, air bubbles whipped or beaten into the ingredients and steam created by the evaporation of the liquids in the batter.

Recipes can also use a combination of both chemical leaveners: baking powder and baking soda. Be sure to use baking soda or baking powder, whichever is specifically called for in the recipe, because they are very different. Swapping them without adjustment is a fast way to cupcake

· · · · · · · · · · · · · · · · · · · · · · · · · · · · · · · · · · · · · · · · · · · · · · · · · · ·

ruin. There are also two types of baking powder: regular or double acting. Whether baking soda or baking powder is used depends on the other ingredients in the recipe. You are about to learn these and all the other secrets behind creating unforgettable cupcakes, and even how to design your own cupcake recipes from the ground up.

## How to Ensure Light, Fluffy Cupcakes

Following is a list of all the things you can do to ensure your cupcakes turn out light, fluffy and unforgettable. Use the techniques below that will work with the cupcake recipe you are using.

- Bring butter to room temperature before adding ingredients.
- Cream the butter until pale yellow before you add the sugar.
- Scrape the sides of the bowl a few times while creaming the butter and sugar together.
- Mix the fat and sugar together until any sugar crystals are dissolved. Superfine sugar has smaller crystals which dissolve faster.
- Bring eggs to room temperature before you add them into the light, fluffy sugar-butter mixture.
- Beat the egg whites with your hand or stand mixer until they form peaks, and fold them in as the last step to completing your batter after the dry ingredients are already combined. Start with ¼ of

the egg whites and mix with a wooden spoon, then mix in the rest just until combined.

- Add your egg yolks one at a time to the sugar-butter mixture; beat or mix in between.
- Don't add your eggs to the batter all at once.
- If you do not separate the eggs and add them separately as detailed above, at least mix them until fluffy.
- Sift your flour and leavening agent (baking soda or baking powder) together. (Sift 2 – 3 times for best results.)
- Make sure your baking powder is fresh.
- Add the dry ingredients a bit at a time, not all at once.
- Don't just add a bunch of ingredients into a bowl and mix.
- Make sure the oven is at the correct temperature using a $5 oven thermometer available everywhere. An oven that is too hot can cause the air bubble pockets to burst and your cupcakes to lose your carefully added bubbles. The cupcakes will then collapse. An oven that is too cold can prevent the cupcakes from rising high enough and get hot enough to set the batter, resulting in collapsed centers.

## The Closely Guarded Secret of Cupcakeaholics

Do you know why closet Cupcakeaholics prefer to make cupcakes from box mixes? Read on to find out. You might think a Cupcakeaholic is a snooty, cupcake elitist. In some

Many people use box cake mixes for years before venturing into the made-from-scratch homemade realm. However, with all the secrets to making cupcakes from scratch right here in the book you are reading, you can jump right to the professional level even if you've never baked anything before in your entire life.

cases, you might be correct. In most cases, you may be surprised to discover Cupcakeaholics prefer to make their cupcakes from box mix. Whoa, step back, Jack; it's true.

The box versus homemade debate isn't always about taste. Box mixes are easy to flavor and whip up, and produce consistently light, fluffy cupcakes. No one but someone with a professional palate can tell box mix cupcakes from cupcakes made from scratch.

Professional Cupcakeaholics will tell you that it only takes a minute to jazz up a box mix into a stunning taste sensation even the experts can't tell. Yes, you're going to discover how to do this.

## Homemade Mixes

Homemade cupcakes (made from scratch) take longer to mix and can be denser and blander than their cake mix counterparts, if you don't know all the little tricks.

Vanilla or other flavor extracts added to the batter add hints of sophisticated flavor and cover up artificial ones that are the giveaway to cupcakes made from a box mix. Flavor extracts also help solve the problem of cupcake mixes that come out with a thicker, drier consistency.

Making your cupcakes from scratch allows for the most personalization, and also requires the most ingredients, has the longest preparation time, and requires that a recipe be followed exactly for the right results. Many people use box cake mixes for years before venturing into the made-from-scratch homemade realm. However, with all the secrets to making cupcakes from scratch right here in the book you are reading, you can jump right to the professional level even if you've never baked anything before in your entire life.

Cupcakes made from scratch allow you to get really creative and invent something wonderful that no one else has ever created. A prepackaged cake mix only allows you to add to what is already there. You can use fresh, whole, organic ingredients like flour, butter, and sugar. Cupcakes can be made even healthier by substituting part of the flour with quinoa, or pastry or whole wheat cake flour. You can even add fruits for flavor, moisture and texture. Oh, it gets better!

## Box Mixes

Most commercial mixes contain additives, hydrogenated fats, artificial colorings and flavorings, preservatives, and lots of sodium. These commercial cake mix additives make for easy, less expensive, quick mixtures that are hard to mess up.

There are recipes in between the two that use a boxed cake mix as a base to which you add other ingredients. A French vanilla cake mixed as directed with some graham cracker crumbs, chocolate kisses, and marshmallow crème can end up as a delicious S'more cupcake batch.

The biggest draw to using cake mix enhanced recipes is that they require fewer ingredients than cupcakes

These commercial cake mix additives make for easy, less expensive, quick mixtures that are hard to mess up.

How do you adapt a cake mix to make cupcakes? The only thing you need to change is the baking time.

made completely from scratch. They incorporate the light and fluffy nature of boxed cake mixes into the cupcakes, they are simple to make and you can still personalize the final results.

How do you adapt a cake mix to make cupcakes? The only thing you need to change is the baking time. You can halve the baking time for most cakes if you make them into cupcakes. Be sure to check your cupcakes at around the 20-minute mark so they don't get overbaked.

Most boxed cake mixes involve only 4 steps:

1. Preheat the oven to 350°F, 177°C.
2. Place paper cup liners into your cupcake pan or muffin tin wells.
3. Prepare batter as directed on the box and pour batter into cups.
4. Bake 20-22 minutes or until done.

You can easily see why cake mix cupcakes are convenient, easy to make and hard to mess up.

The endless varieties of cake mixes available allow you to experiment with a wide variety of flavors without having to purchase numerous ingredients. This makes boxed cake mixes less expensive than baking cupcakes from scratch. Early cake mixes were not readily embraced because they didn't taste as good as from-scratch varieties and produced inconsistent results. All that has changed.

The quality of cake mixes has improved dramatically over the last few decades and today more cakes and cupcakes are made from prepackaged mixes than from scratch. Some people prefer the taste of cake mixes and find them moister and lighter in texture, while others think that they have an odd aftertaste. This aftertaste is particularly evident in yellow cake mixes.

What's the secret to getting rid of the odd taste that can be the giveaway that you used a boxed cake mix? You can add a bit of dry sherry, pure almond extract, or lime zest. Which one and how much depends on how sensitive your taste buds are to the artificial taste, and how much artificial taste is in the mix. I like to use two teaspoons (10 ml) of fresh lemon juice along with a teaspoon (5 ml) of lemon zest. Lime also works nicely. You don't usually need to reduce the other liquids by the same amount, but you can experiment with your mix to see if it makes a difference. The more you neutralize the artificial taste, and the more fresh ingredients you add, the closer the box mix will taste to homemade.

Why do many Cupcakeaholics prefer to use a box mix and personalize the mix from there? Because box mixes are quicker to blend, bake, eat – and hide or destroy the evidence than cupcakes made from scratch.

You may also want to consider using organic ingredients with a regular cake mix or with an organic cake mix. Organic cupcakes don't contain ingredients contaminated by chemicals, preservatives, trans fats, artificial coloring and additives, and hydrogenated oil. Some bakers find organic ingredients make for a purer flavor. Since not everyone has the budget that will bear organic and exotic ingredients, you will find your results are most affected by the freshness of your other

You can add a bit of dry sherry, pure almond extract, or lime zest.

Because box mixes are quicker to blend, bake, eat – and hide or destroy the evidence than cupcakes made from scratch.

Freshness is a key factor in choosing ingredients to make your cupcakes.

Remember that the most important factor in choosing your ingredients is the freshness of the ingredients.

ingredients and the method you use to mix the batter. Freshness is a key factor in choosing ingredients to make your cupcakes.

All regular ingredients can be replaced with organic ones. Organic vanilla extract, unrefined organic caster sugar, organic flours and cocoa powders, organic butters/organic non-hydrogenated butter substitutes, organic eggs, and organic fruits for garnish or juice.

Organic ingredients don't automatically make a cupcake healthy food. Substituting hard-core "healthy" ingredients could change the flavor of cupcakes by making them taste grainy and like the twigs and berry health food my daughters roll their eyes at. In some circles, making cupcakes healthy ruins the whole point of cupcakes.

Whether the taste crosses the line depends on how you substitute healthy ingredients in a cupcake recipe. It is possible to make cupcakes so the consistency and texture are nearly identical. A key difference is in the preference of the baker and in the consideration of the allergies, food sensitivities and taste buds of the person who will ultimately eat the cupcake. Some cupcake fans love tons of sugary frosting and some scrape it all off just for the cake.

Whether you choose to make your cupcakes from scratch, semi-scratch, or from a box mix, and whether you use organic or traditional ingredients is entirely a matter of personal choice. Any of these can be used to make unforgettable cupcakes. Remember that the most important factor in choosing your ingredients is the freshness of the ingredients.

## How Professional Pastry Chefs Create Unforgettable Cupcakes: Their Secret Ritual

One of the little known secrets the professional pastry chefs use to create perfection every time is simple to do. It's so simple most people blow it off because they are rushed. Yet, if you take the time to read through the ingredient list and the entire recipe to make sure you understand all the steps of the recipe and visualize how it will come together, you can join the league of the award-winning cupcake bakers. Even if you invented the recipe, taking a minute to read through your own instructions can ensure your own gold medal results every time.

These extra few minutes allow you to be sure all the ingredients are available, are at the proper temperature, and are combined in the correct order. You minimize the chance of mistakes or surprises. This can mean the difference between a good cupcake and a cupcake of pure bliss.

If you take the time to read through the ingredient list and the entire recipe to make sure you understand all the steps of the recipe and visualize how it will come together, you can join the league of the award-winning cupcake bakers.

*Chapter 4*

# The Distance between Disappointment and Divine

The distance between disappointment and divine can often be measured, literally. How precisely you measure your ingredients will affect the final baked results. If you don't measure the ingredients precisely you can end up with dry, flat, uninspiring creations or lumpy messes destined for the garbage can.

The United States originally adopted the British system of weights and measures, although the systems branched away from each other in the 1800s. The Brits continued to measure based on weights, and the Americans adopted volume measurements instead.

Early measurements of flour and sugar by the teacup combined with a certain number of eggs were quick, easy and much cheaper than acquiring an accurate scale. I'm betting the scales were all enlisted to weigh the gold being mined out in the Wild, Wild West. That's just a guess, but something tells me that simple economics would raise the demand and thus, the price of available scales. Back then real gold was more valuable than a cupcake. Can you believe it?

Early measurements of flour and sugar by the teacup combined with a certain number of eggs were quick, easy and much cheaper than acquiring an accurate scale.

Precise measurements are what can give you professional cupcake bakery results the very first time you try to bake any recipe. Precision can take you to the top quickly.

Needless to say, measurements by reference to butter that was the size of an egg, also called a "knob" of butter, and less than precise measurements resulted in varying degrees of baking success until the baker acquired a healthy amount of experience.

Today, professional bakers even in America often use a scale to weigh flour and other bulk ingredients. However, most recipes in cupcake books call for volume measurements. Just in case you run into an unforgettable recipe on the Internet that uses the measuring system opposite of what you are used to, you will be able to convert the recipe into your system, and even understand the system behind it.

What is important is to precisely measure the ingredients as they are listed in the recipe. Precise measurements are what can give you professional cupcake bakery results the very first time you try to bake any recipe. Precision can take you to the top quickly.

Since cupcake recipes usually include flour in the greatest volume for any single ingredient, it is frequently the easiest ingredient to measure incorrectly if you are using a new recipe.

In the "Cupcake Making Tools" section, you will find a complete list of the tools you need to correctly measure the ingredients. In short, dry ingredients should be measured in nesting/dry measuring cups and leveled with a knife or spatula. Wet ingredients should be measured by carefully pouring the exact amount into a glass measuring cup.

Wet and dry measuring cups really are different. Wet measures have a ledge above the measurement line to prevent spilling. Dry ingredients such as flour and sugar compact when tapped to settle at the desired line. Too much of one ingredient may adversely affect the recipe. Measuring liquids in a dry measure is fine, although it may be a bit more difficult to pour without spilling.

## Pre-Baking Rituals
## (before you crack a single egg)

Like lighting the candles for a romantic interlude in any great love affair, pre-baking rituals are steps a baker takes before cracking a single egg or measuring a cup or gram of flour. These pre-baking preparations are often the difference between the bliss of a perfect, moist cupcake and a distasteful dry crummy mess. The preparation step is often ignored or breezed over, even though it is critical to the overall baking process.

Preparation includes: preheating the oven, selecting the proper baking equipment, greasing the pan, and gathering supplies and ingredients.

Always test a recipe before a big event. Please re-read that last sentence. Variables such as oven temperature, ingredient quality, preparation techniques, and bake time affect the final product, so it's best to perfect this combination without the pressure of a looming party where your cupcakes have to make a command performance.

Too much of one ingredient may adversely affect the recipe.

Always test a recipe before a big event.

Variables such as oven temperature, ingredient quality, preparation techniques, and bake time affect the final product, so it's best to perfect this combination without the pressure of a looming party where your cupcakes have to make a command performance.

Organize all the ingredients and baking tools before starting. Carefully check to see if there is enough of each ingredient and set them in an easily accessible location. Eggs and butter should be brought out of the refrigerator at this time and allowed to warm to room temperature before you mix the batter. Skipping this step and using them cold is the reason many cupcakes don't turn out right, and you may never realize why. Gather the mixing bowl, mixer, spatula, measuring cups and spoons, and baking pans. Just like planning a delicious banquet, the baking process should begin hours before an event so that the cupcakes will have plenty of time to bake, cool, and get dressed.

I know organization does not sound like fun; however, you will find that as in any successful endeavor, the expression "failure to plan is a plan to fail" applies.

## Ratios Determine Your Results

The types of cake batter traditionally made into cupcakes are classified by the fat-to-flour ratio. The higher the ratio of sugar and fat to flour, the richer the cake. The classification of your cake will determine the method you use to mix the cake. The method used to mix your cupcake batter is critical to truly scrumptious cupcakes; so don't skip the section on mixing!

## The Perfect Oven Temperature

The perfect oven temperature is vital, too. The ideal for most cupcake recipes is 350°F, 177°C, but always follow the recommendation on the recipe that will be used. Cupcake batter should not be placed in the oven until the oven is thoroughly heated and steadily holding its temperature.

An oven that is too cold or too hot will affect baking times and how the cupcakes rise and brown. An oven thermostat helps you insure that your oven is set at the correct temperature. Pick up an oven thermostat if you don't already have one. For less than a $5 investment, you can save many a batch of overbaked cupcakes.

## Selecting the Perfect Cupcake Tin

Cupcake pan selection is a very personal choice. Muffin tins, which are referred to interchangeably as cupcake tins, are made from a variety of different materials, including aluminum, stainless steel and Silicone. Each type affects how cupcakes bake in different ways. No matter what they're made of, the best cupcake tins should have convenient handles and great heat conductivity. The right metal pan is shiny and sturdy.

Shiny pans reflect heat away and produce lighter-colored crusts. Dark finishes absorb heat more quickly and may lead to overcooked cupcakes. When using a dark pan, it may be necessary to reduce the oven thermostat by 25°F, 17°C.

Pick up an oven thermostat if you don't already have one. For less than a $5 investment, you can save many a batch of overbaked cupcakes.

When using a dark pan, it may be necessary to reduce the oven thermostat by 25°F, 17°C.

Stainless steel muffin tins are not the best heat conductors and often have a copper or aluminum bottom to help distribute heat.

They don't react with food or retain odors, and are lightweight and recyclable.

Most muffin pans are made of lightweight, coated aluminum. Coated aluminum is useful because it is rust resistant and doesn't get hot spots. Insulated aluminum pans slow browning, so cupcakes baked this way might take a bit longer than usual. Darker colored aluminum tins brown cupcakes more quickly, while air-cushioned tins produce smaller, lighter cupcakes. Expensive, heavy aluminum muffin tins don't have any advantages over lightweight versions, nor do they produce superior results. Overall, aluminum bakeware is an excellent and durable option.

Stainless steel is popular in high-end cooking stores and, although often more expensive than other options, is very durable, rust resistant, and will not alter the taste of baked goods. Stainless steel muffin tins are not the best heat conductors, and often have a copper or aluminum bottom to help distribute heat. Most bakers don't recommend stainless steel bakeware because it distributes heat unevenly, which can lead to cupcakes that are overcooked in one area and mushy in another. The copper or aluminum bottoms aim to correct for this stainless steel shortcoming.

Silicone muffin trays and cups were invented as an alternative to metal cookware, which is often coated with potentially hazardous non-stick chemicals like PFOA. Silicone muffin trays are highly flexible and can withstand a huge variety of temperatures. Good quality Silicone muffin trays can be refrigerated, frozen, baked and microwaved. They don't react with food or retain odors, and are lightweight and recyclable. Because they don't absorb heat as do metal muffin tins, the cooking process stops as soon as the tray is removed from the oven. This prevents additional browning on the bottom and sides of cupcakes. Silicone cookware is more expensive. The major complaint bakers have about Silicone is that cupcakes can be difficult to remove. Silicone is also floppy, must be supported by a baking sheet and there are no long-term studies supporting or disavowing its health affects and safety.

## How to Ensure Easy Cupcake Removal

Easy cupcake removal is important. There are three ways to bake cupcakes and keep them from sticking to the pan.
1.  In a metal muffin pan with paper or foil cups
2.  In a metal muffin pan without cup liners
3.  In a Silicone muffin tray or in Silicone cups on a cookie sheet

Paper baking cups are easy to use, keep cupcakes fresher longer, make it easy to remove baked goods from the pan, and eliminate the need for grease or spray. They come in many different patterns and colors. You can dress cupcakes up or down for each occasion. When using paper cups, make sure to spread them evenly throughout the pan and remove paper separators from foil cup liners before adding batter.

Even if you use cupcake liners, most cupcake tins are prepared before use in order to keep cupcakes from sticking to the pan. This keeps the cupcakes easy to remove,

Paper baking cups are easy to use, keep cupcakes fresher longer, make it easy to remove baked goods from the pan, and eliminate the need for grease or spray.

For chocolate cupcakes, the muffin tins can be coated with one of the same oils of your choice and dusted with cocoa powder so that the cupcakes won't have white residue on their walls.

and cleanup is a cinch once they come out of the oven. The cupcake tin can be prepared by coating it with melted shortening, coconut oil, or butter, and sprinkled with powdered sugar or flour. For chocolate cupcakes, the muffin tins can be coated with one of the same oils of your choice and dusted with cocoa powder so that the cupcakes won't have white residue on their walls. Non-stick pans should never be greased with vegetable oil spray because it leaves a residue.

Most bakers prefer to prepare their pans with shortening, which doesn't burn easily or leave a funny taste. Butter is a good option as well, although it makes for a darker, thicker crust. Baker's grease works well, but must be mixed before use. Even better (except for non-stick pans), use this cupcake pan coating secret: There is a special kind of cooking spray that combines oil and flour and makes coating pans (other than non-stick) the perfect choice. Pam offers this in their special "Baking" spray, Baker's Joy; and Crisco also offers sprays with this amazing combination. If you are baking for gluten-free clients, these options won't work. Instead, use paper liners or coat the cupcake wells with Crisco and dust powdered sugar in them.

Silicone cups and trays should be prepared with non-stick spray or shortening and placed on a level cookie sheet before adding batter, so when the cupcakes have baked and cooled, they can be removed from Silicone cups by turning them upside down and gently pressing the bottom of each cup while peeling away the sides.

Preparation is especially important for Silicone since the number one complaint with them is that the cupcakes stick to the Silicone cups and are impossible to remove without destroying the cupcakes.

When the oven is preheated and the cooking supplies have been gathered, it's time to prepare the ingredients.

Silicone cups and trays should be prepared with non-stick spray or shortening and placed on a level cookie sheet before adding batter, so when the cupcakes have baked and cooled, they can be removed from Silicone cups by turning them upside down and gently pressing the bottom of each cup while peeling away the sides.

Part 2:

# THE BEST
# CUPCAKE
*Ingredients*

*Chapter 5*

# Introduction to Cupcake Ingredients

Ingredients can make or break a recipe. The basic ingredients of plain, white cupcakes are butter or shortening, flour, sugar, baking powder, salt, egg, milk, and vanilla extract. Recipes vary by type and flavor, but many of the ingredients stay the same.

No matter which recipe you use, the ingredients must be fresh. The freshness of the ingredients you use is so important that nothing will rescue cupcakes made from ingredients that have rounded the top of the age hill. People, like wine, get better with age. Cupcake ingredients do not. In fact, your hard work will end up in the trash can if you use expired ingredients, no matter if you did it accidentally or thought you could get away with it just this once. So let's look at how you test for freshness.

Your first step is fast and easy: smell and taste your ingredients. If they smell or taste bad, you definitely don't need to test any further.

Next, let's examine each of the ingredients, one by one, in the next chapters.

The freshness of the ingredients you use is so important that nothing will rescue cupcakes made from ingredients that have rounded the top of the age hill.

*Chapter 6*

# Flours

Your main enemies of flour are bugs, oxygenation and moisture.

## Testing Your Stored Flour for Freshness

Rancid flour tastes sharp, bitter or just plain "off." Rancid flour also smells strange, like something you don't want to eat. Be prepared to spit if you're testing flour that has been sitting on a shelf in your kitchen and you don't know or remember when you bought it.

## Shopping for Fresh Flour

Look at the "use by date" on the flour first. If there is a series of dates available among the packages on the shelf, buy the flour with the date as far ahead as possible.

Examine the packaging for signs of bug infestation. A spider web type material in crevices or tiny holes in the packaging is a sign of potential hitchhikers that could not only ruin your cupcakes, but infest your whole kitchen. If you don't find these signs until after you get home, there are a few steps you can take or do to prevent a problem developing from eggs that could be present even in the

If there is a series of dates available among the packages on the shelf, buy the flour with the date as far ahead as possible.

75

absence of other visible evidence of bugs, dead or alive. Since some bugs and bug larvae can be microscopic, it is a great idea to take the following steps when bringing home flour.

Open your flour and put it in an airtight freezer safe container. Once you open the flour, you can inspect the flour as you transfer it to the container.

If you don't find anything in the flour that would cause you to return it to the store for refund, put the airtight container with the flour into the freezer. Four days in the freezer should kill any microscopic living organisms or eggs that could escape visual inspection. The University of Texas at Austin reports even the hardiest insects and insect eggs will be killed with an exposure to 14° to 40°F degrees Fahrenheit (-10° to 4° degrees Celsius) over a 25-day period. So if you want to be 100% certain, you can freeze the flour for 25 days.

Alternatively, you can remove the oxygen by using an oxygen absorbing packet and store in the freezer or refrigerator in an airtight container, or use dry ice and store in the freezer. Sift your flour before adding it to your cupcake recipe. This will eliminate egg remains if there are any.

If you purchase flour to use right away, and based on a visual inspection you don't find any bugs, you can skip the freezing process. That's because once you heat flour up to 130° Fahrenheit (55° Celsius) during the cupcake baking process, any tiny insects or eggs that may have escaped notice will be killed.

## How to Store Flour to Extend Freshness

You can also preserve and extend the freshness of flour by storing it in the freezer until you are ready to use it. Proper airtight freezer storage can extend the life of white, bleached flour almost indefinitely.

- Whole grain and alternative flours (whole wheat, barley, oat, rye, quinoa, spelt, etc.) contain natural fats of the grain or nut and are more susceptible to spoiling by becoming rancid over time.

    Store these flours in a sealed airtight container in the freezer for three to six months from the purchase date.
    - Label the container with the purchase date.
    - Bring up to room temperature before using.
    - Do not store at room temperature. Even at cool room temperature, these flours don't last long after opened. If you are purchasing them for baking within the next week or two, then you're fine!
    - If purchased in a plastic bag, you can store in a cool, dark place until the expiration date stamped at the factory.

- White flour includes all purpose, self-rising, cake and pastry flours.

    Store these white flours in a sealed airtight container in the freezer for up to two years from

Whole grain and alternative flours contain natural fats of the grain or nut and are more susceptible to spoiling by becoming rancid over time.

It's the reason you don't want to use 100% whole wheat flour for baking cupcakes.

the purchase date, and up to eight months in a cool, dry dark cupboard.

- Label the container with the purchase date.
- Bring up to room temperature before using.
- Seal white flours in recipe-sized portions in airtight freezer bags for convenience of use. This will avoid continual exposure to room temperature air if you plan on storing flour for a long period of time.

Whichever flour you are storing, as long as you seal the flour in plastic to protect it from absorbing moisture and odors, the flour will last longer in the refrigerator and freezer.

## Finding Just the Right Cupcake Flour

The goal of most cupcake baking endeavors is a light, moist cupcake that dances on your tongue. Know your way around the varieties of flours and which ones you can use in cupcakes to get the right result.

The key differences in how varieties of flour perform in your cupcake recipes are in taste and protein content. The protein or gluten content of flour is the key to the strength and the structure of the final baked product. The higher the protein (gluten) content, the greater the strength and elasticity.

This is the reason you get chewier, denser cupcakes with flours high in protein. It's the reason you don't want to use 100% whole wheat flour for baking cupcakes.

Flours are classified into two primary types: hard and soft. The hard flours are high in gluten (protein). These are the flours used in breads and result in a dense, chewy texture. Soft flours are low in gluten (low in protein) and are the type used in cupcakes, cakes and other light pastries.

Even among hard and soft flours there are many different varieties. Cupcakes made with different types of flour will have different tastes and textures. If a recipe calls for cake flour, you won't get the same results from all-purpose flour. Using higher protein (gluten) types of flours will result in chewy, dense creations that are better suited to substituting for the puck in a hockey game.

Here's the rundown so you can avoid the rink unless your favorite local hockey team runs out of real pucks and you WANT to help them out.

All-purpose flour is the most common type called for in cupcake recipes. However, many bakers believe that cake flour is the best choice. All-purpose and cake flour can be purchased in organic/non-bleached varieties. Bleached flour is more processed than the organic varieties.

Cake flour is milled from soft wheat with lower levels of gluten and protein and creates finer, airier cupcakes. Some recipes call for sifted flour. Even if sifting isn't required, it doesn't hurt to sift. Sifting flour leads to lighter cupcakes because it aerates the flour and removes any lumps or foreign particles.

Whole wheat flour is a healthy alternative to processed white flour since whole wheat flour is higher in B vitamins,

Cake flour is milled from soft wheat with lower levels of gluten and protein and creates finer, airier cupcakes.

If you don't have cake flour on hand, you can substitute ¾ cup all purpose flour (90 g/3.17 oz) plus 2 Tbsp. (30 g) of cornstarch for each cup (104 g/3.67 oz) of cake flour.

minerals and vitamin E, as well as fiber. Regular whole wheat flour will give a dense texture not suitable for light crumb. Even the whole wheat pastry flour changes the taste and texture of the cupcake too. It makes the cake denser and taste much less like a dessert.

Whole wheat pastry flour is milled from soft wheat, contains less gluten (protein) than regular whole wheat flour, and results in a more tender final product. While using exclusively whole wheat pastry flour can still result in dense, grainy cupcakes, using half whole wheat pastry flour and half cake flour, regular pastry flour, or even all-purpose flour can increase health benefits without altering the taste too dramatically. Plus, a ½ substitution will make the whole grain "improvement" undetectable to cupcake eaters.

Since cake flour is designed specifically for cake, it will give you a lighter result. If you don't have cake flour on hand, you can substitute ¾ cup all purpose flour (90 g/3.17 oz) plus 2 Tbsp. (30 g) of cornstarch for each cup (104 g/3.67 oz) of cake flour.

European wheat flour is lower in gluten (protein) than the wheat flour in the United States, so check carefully for the country of origin of your flour. If you are using European flour, you may need to add an extra egg or two to reinforce the structure of the cake.

Don't let this stop you from experimenting with other kinds of flours or adapting other kinds of cake or muffin recipes that have other pleasurable textures. Some of the most memorable affairs result from happy adventures off the beaten path. See the Flour & Flour Substitute Weight,

Measurement and Nutrition Equivalent Chart on page 81.

## The Heartbreak that Hides in the Flour

Even a slight variance in the amount of flour can make a huge difference between the forgettable and unforgettable. Between bliss and bomb. Measuring the ingredients precisely is the key. How you measure the flour in your cupcake recipes is crucial.

Unless the recipe specifically tells you to measure the flour any other way, then regardless of the type of flour called for in the recipe, use the "stir and spoon method": gently stir the flour to aerate it before you carefully spoon the flour into a dry measuring cup (if you are measuring by volume instead of weight). Then take the flat edge of a kitchen knife and draw it across the edge of the measuring cup to level off your measurement. All-purpose flour measured this way weighs four and a half ounces.

Many methods of measuring flour that work fine for cookies or shortbreads can set cupcake batter on the road to ruin. Ways NOT to measure flour? Don't scoop the flour out directly with the measuring cup and don't press, pack or tap flour in the measuring cup.

Deviate from measuring flour this way <u>only</u> if the recipe says so or specifically calls for a different method of measuring. Want a lighter, fluffier cupcake? Sift your flour after you measure it.

Many methods of measuring flour that work fine for cookies or shortbreads can set cupcake batter on the road to ruin.

## When to Sift the Flour

Knowing this is the difference between failure and success.

Whether or not you should sift flour before or after measuring the flour depends on where the word "sift" or "sifted" appears.

- If a cupcake recipe calls for "3 cups of sifted flour," sift the flour first, then measure it.
- If the cupcake recipe calls for "3 cups flour, sifted," then measure first, and sift after you measure.

Sifting before or after affects the amount of flour that ends up in the recipe. Even a small amount of difference can dramatically affect the moisture, structure and tenderness of the finished cupcakes.

## Flours Not Made for Unforgettable Cupcakes

- Bread Flour – Don't use any bread flours. Substituting these flours for regular flour will result in chewy cupcakes.
- Whole Wheat Flour – Higher in protein than bread flour, whole wheat flour will not make good cupcakes. If you want to include some whole wheat flour, use whole wheat pastry flour to substitute for $1/3$ to no more than $1/3$ of the flour called for in the recipe for best results.
- Self-Rising Flour – Not recommended unless the

recipe was designed for it. If you must use it in a pinch, then don't add the baking powder or baking soda. Self-rising flour already includes baking powder in the amount needed to leaven the flour you use.

If a recipe calls for self-rising flour and you want to substitute a different flour, just add 1-1/2 teaspoons (7.5 ml) of baking powder and 1/2 tsp. (3 g) of salt per approximately each cup (120 g/4.23 oz) of flour.

The higher the protein percentage in the flour, the denser the structure.

## Protein Percentages in Flour

| Type of Flour | Percent Protein |
|---:|:---|
| Cake | 7 – 9% |
| All-Purpose | 10 – 11% |
| Bread | 11 – 13% |
| Whole Wheat | 13.5 – 15% |

Don't let this stop you from experimenting with other kinds of flours or adapting other kinds of cake or muffin recipes that have other pleasurable textures. Some of the most memorable affairs result from happy adventures off the beaten path.

When you start to look for ways to create amazing cupcakes outside the bounds of the hallowed halls of kitchen chemistry, the place to start is flavor.

It is easier than you think to leave behind the high fat, high gluten and sugar spiking ingredients for healthier choices.

## How Gluten-Free, Vegan and Healthier Cupcakes Can Taste Unforgettable (in a blissful way)

When you start to look for ways to create amazing cupcakes outside the bounds of the hallowed halls of kitchen chemistry, the place to start is flavor. There are endless cupcake recipes in the vegan, gluten-free, sugar-free and fat-free categories that could taste amazing if flavor was a requirement to begin with.

Most cupcake recipes are stripped of their flavor during the process of trying to make them fit into a particular diet and texture, sometimes to the point of removing any reason to eat them at all. That doesn't need to be the case if you use the guidelines in this book to adapt cupcake recipes.

If you're craving a cupcake, will eating something that "almost" tastes like a cupcake fill your craving? Or will it leave you feeling only half satisfied so that you eat twice as many and then break down to get a "real" cupcake in the end, anyway? Personally, I don't want to hear the little voice in my head mock me, so I start with flavor. You might be surprised how sinfully delicious a cupcake that starts by focusing on flavor can be.

The easiest place to start is in the gluten-free category. It is easier than you think to leave behind the high fat, high gluten and sugar spiking ingredients for healthier choices.

There are a multitude of gluten-free flour substitutes available. The gluten-free flour substitute mix recipes that follow are free of gluten, wheat, soy, corn, potato, peanuts, tree nuts, and dairy.

Why not just gluten-free? That answer is easy. Frequently, people who are sensitive to gluten are also sensitive to one or more of these other ingredients. Maybe you just want to make healthier cupcakes. I love my cupcakes made with brown rice flour and quinoa because they are so much healthier than white, processed flour and my taste buds love them, too!

- Simple Gluten-Free Cupcake Flour Substitute Mix Option A
  (Easy to have these three GF flours on hand)
  - 1 cup (160 grams) brown rice flour
  - 1 cup (136 grams) sorghum flour
  - 1 cup (120 grams) tapioca starch
- Gluten-Free Cupcake Flour Substitute Mix Option B
  - 2 cups (320 grams) brown rice flour
  - 1/4 cup plus 2 Tbsp. (48 grams) arrowroot
  - 1/3 cup (40 grams) tapioca starch/a.k.a. tapioca flour
- Gluten-Free Flour Substitute Mix Option C
  - 1 cup (160 grams) brown rice flour
  - 1 cup (136 grams) sorghum flour
  - 1/4 cup plus 2 Tbsp. (48 grams) arrowroot

Brown rice flour and quinoa are whole grains packed with more nutrition and protein than other flour types, including other non-gluten flours.

1/3 cup quinoa flour (40.7 grams)

1 tsp. (3 grams) xanthan gum

Instructions for the mixes above:

Brown rice flour and quinoa are whole grains packed with more nutrition and protein than other flour types, including other non-gluten flours. Brown rice settles to the bottom of the mix so you must shake, mix and whisk well prior to each use.

You can substitute 1 cup (160 grams/5.64 ounces) of white rice flour for the 1 cup (136 grams/4.8 ounces) of sorghum flour.

You can also substitute tapioca, almond, buckwheat, or coconut flours for the quinoa. Keep substitutions to 1/3 cup (or below 50 grams/1.76 ounces) in the recipe above if you want light, fluffy results, otherwise ride the experimental high. Just keep in mind adding the denser flours such as quinoa, almond, buckwheat or coconut flours create denser consistency.

Make sure you whisk and thoroughly stir the flours until they are extremely well combined.

## Health Benefits of Non-Gluten Flours

### Quinoa Flour

You can substitute half the flour called for in the recipe with quinoa flour. Quinoa (pronounced KEEN-WAH) is the healthiest grain available because it is the closest to being a perfect protein source from plants. The balance of nutrition inside the plant, including 20% protein, trumps the 2% protein content of wheat flour.

Quinoa flour is ground from the seeds of a plant similar to spinach. It is a source of all essential amino acids and has a range of essential vitamins and other nutrients. It's probably one of the best ways to make your cupcakes healthier. Remember, you can only substitute up to half the flour with quinoa because quinoa does not contain the gluten to support the structure of the cake. There are also ways to use quinoa in gluten-free baking mixes in a smaller amount. (See the baking gluten-free cupcakes section.) Bob's Red Mill makes an excellent quinoa flour. It's available at health food stores and online at Amazon.com.

### Brown Rice Flour

Brown rice flour is gluten-free and chock full of the vitamins and all the nutrients that are stripped out of white flours. While many brown rice flours can give baked goods a gritty taste, Bob's Red Mill Organic Brown Rice Flour is one of my gluten-free "go to" ingredients without the gritty taste. I love it and use it frequently in my gluten-free cupcake mixes.

*Chapter 7*

# The Magic of Emulsifiers in Cupcakes

Emulsifiers are the Cyrano de Bergeracs of cupcake batter. They do all their work behind the scenes and without them, there's nothing. Cupcakes without the proper emulsifiers are chewy, tough, and dry, inedible and unforgettable for all the wrong reasons. Without emulsifiers, the fat in the batter is unevenly distributed and the finished cupcake is also oily.

Emulsifiers stabilize the batter and improve the consistency and texture of the cupcake. They bind ingredients that would normally remain separate in a mixture. Think of oil and water. An emulsifier is like the chemical equivalent of an aphrodisiac for oil and water so they cuddle closely together until they can be bound together permanently in the heat of the oven. Emulsifiers also coat and strengthen the protein structures in the batter. Emulsifiers allow the air bubbles in the mixture to expand without breaking. They form complexes within the starch molecules and retard the firming rate during the baking process, producing a more tender crumb. Emulsifiers also increase and help evenly distribute the number of air bubbles in the batter to stabilize the batter.

Commercial cake mixes usually include soy lecithin, a powdered emulsifier. Lecithin occurs naturally in egg yolks and can be extracted from soy.

Emulsifiers are the Cyrano de Bergeracs of cupcake batter. They do all their work behind the scenes and without them, there's nothing.

*Chapter 8*

# Leavening Your Cupcakes

## Baking Soda in Cupcake Recipes

Baking soda, also known as sodium bicarbonate, is a powerful chemical leavener used to develop the volume of the batter to produce the light, tender crumb of the cupcake. Known as an alkali, it neutralizes acids in the cupcake batter. Baking soda is one of the few alkalis in cupcake baking. Other alkalis include egg whites and Dutch processed powder.

Baking soda is one side of the leavening equation. Too much baking soda added to a cupcake recipe will leave a bitter taste unless countered by the acidity of other ingredients, like buttermilk, lemon or lime juice, molasses, brown sugar, sour cream or honey. As soon as baking soda is added to the batter, it begins to work. Remember that because baking soda starts working immediately, it does not need the oven to begin the process of rising the batter. This means you need to put the cupcakes into the oven to bake as soon as possible.

What happens if the cupcake batter sits out for a while? The cupcakes could fall flat. Hockey puck, anyone? If the recipe calls for baking soda, you cannot substitute baking

Too much baking soda added to a cupcake recipe will leave a bitter taste unless countered by the acidity of other ingredients, like buttermilk, lemon or lime juice, molasses, brown sugar, sour cream or honey.

If the recipe calls for baking soda, you cannot substitute baking powder without adjusting the recipe. Baking soda is four times more powerful than baking powder.

When creating or checking your cupcake recipes, the rule of thumb is to use ¼ tsp. (1 g) of baking soda for every 1 cup (120 g/4.23 oz) of flour.

powder without adjusting the recipe. Baking soda is 4 times more powerful than baking powder. If you did try to directly substitute baking soda for baking powder without adjustments, you would over-leaven the batter, causing the batter to rise to the point where the little pockets of air rise too much and burst, leaving you with bitter tasting cupcakes that could substitute for paper weights. All you would need is a coat of shellac.

When creating or checking your cupcake recipes, the rule of thumb is to use ¼ tsp. (1 g) of baking soda for every 1 cup (120 g/4.23 oz) of flour.

## Is Baking Powder Better than Baking Soda?

Baking powder has two active ingredients: cream of tartar (tartaric acid) and baking soda (sodium bicarbonate). Single-acting baking powder is like baking soda in its reaction. It must be baked immediately, too, because it is activated by moisture and starts working as soon as it is added to the batter.

Double-acting baking powder is a bit different. Double-acting baking powder works in two phases and can be left out for awhile. Some of it starts working as soon as it's added to the batter, but most of its work is performed as it reacts with the hot oven. Baking powder contains both an acid and a base and results in a neutral flavor. It's commonly used in cupcakes, cakes and biscuits. Make sure that the baking powder or baking soda is fresh, because if it is past its expiration date, the cupcakes may not rise properly.

If the recipe calls for baking powder, the rule of thumb is 1 tsp. (4 g) of single acting baking powder or 2/3 tsp. (2.67 g) of double-acting baking powder for every 1 cup (120 g/4.23 oz) of flour.

## How to Test Your Chemical Leaveners for Freshness

To test baking soda for freshness: Add 1/4 tsp. (1 g) of baking soda to 2 tsp. (10 ml) of vinegar or lemon juice. Fresh baking soda will bubble quickly.

To test baking powder for freshness: Add 1 tsp. (4 g) of baking powder to 1/3 cup (79 ml) of hot water. Hot tap water is fine for this test. The baking powder is fresh if the mixture hisses or fizzes.

*Chapter 9*

# The Role of Butter, Shortenings and Oils in Creating Unforgettable Cupcakes

Butter and shortenings carry flavors, help make the cupcake tender by coating the protein in the flour and also add to the light, delicate texture by cradling the air bubbles until the oven seals them in the finished product.

In most cases, shortening, oil, and butter cannot be used interchangeably without adjusting the recipe and/or the amounts. If liquid oil is used in place of a solid fat like oil or butter, the amount of other liquids used should be decreased. If the recipe calls for melted butter, you can substitute liquid oil in equal amounts.

If butter is used instead of shortening, less should be used because butter contains more liquid than shortening. The addition of butter to the recipe also calls for a decrease in the amount of other liquids used.

Regular margarine can be substituted one part for one part for butter. The taste will be different in cupcakes made with margarine and many bakers do not use margarine because they find it alters the flavor and mouth feel too much.

Margarines and Buttery Spreads with less than 60% fat are not designed to be used in baking.

Margarine that contains less than 80% fat or has the words "light," "low fat," "lower fat," "reduced fat," "lower or reduced calories," "diet," "vegetable oil," "vegetable spread," or "fat free" are more difficult to substitute for butter in baking. Products labeled this way contain a high quantity of water and much lower quantity of fat. Margarines and Buttery Spreads with less than 60% fat are not designed to be used in baking.

There is no exact way to substitute liquid oil for solid fat in a recipe. You will need to adjust other ingredients, particularly liquids when you start to substitute a liquid oil for a solid fat or the other way around. Liquid oil is 100% fat, whereas butter, solid fats and margarines have a lower percentage of fat on a one-to-one basis.

Solid fats include shortening and coconut oil. Shortening is available in vegan and non-hydrogenated forms now. Both help in the process of adding air into the cupcake batter when you whip it with other ingredients like eggs and sugar. Liquid oils present a greater challenge to incorporate the same amount of air bubbles and often result in a heavier, more compact cupcake. For cupcake recipes with a heavier crumb, this is not an issue. If you would like to substitute liquid fat for a solid one, you can do that with the recommended adjustments in the Fat Substitution chart on page 98. Since liquid fat translates into a heavier crumb, you can compensate and add to the lightness of the crumb by whipping your eggs or egg whites separately and folding them in rather than creaming them with the sugar.

The following chart can be referenced as a starting point for fat substitution in cupcake baking. Please keep at the top of your mind that because baking cupcakes is a form of delicate kitchen chemistry, your particular recipe may need additional adjusting. Bottom line: You might not get it right the first time, so please don't attempt substitutions if you are on a deadline to prepare cupcakes for a special occasion. Finding the perfect adjustments to your favorite cupcake recipes is a process without a magic wand. When you do get it right you feel so… wonderful.

Since liquid fat translates into a heavier crumb, you can compensate and add to the lightness of the crumb by whipping your eggs or egg whites separately and folding them in rather than creaming them with the sugar.

## Fat (Butter and Oil Substitution) Chart

| The Recipe Calls For | Substitution |
| --- | --- |
| 1 cup (227 grams) of butter<br>= 2 sticks of butter<br>= 8 ounces<br>= 22 grams | 7/8 cup (207 ml) vegetable or canola oil plus ½ tsp. (3 g) salt |
| | 1 cup regular margarine (227 grams)<br>3/4 cup (178 ml) organic coconut oil |
| | ½ cup (119 ml) applesauce plus ½ cup (113.5 g) of butter |
| | ½ cup pureed or canned pumpkin (119 ml) plus<br>½ cup (113.5 g) butter |
| | ½ cup (119 ml) pureed pears plus ½ cup (113.5 g) butter |
| | ½ cup (119 ml) nonfat yogurt plus ½ cup (113.5 g) butter |
| | ½ cup (119 ml) plain yogurt plus ½ cup (113.5 g) butter |
| | ½ cup (119 ml) pureed dates or prunes plus ½ cup (113.5 g) butter |
| | ½ cup applesauce (119 ml) plus ½ cup (119 ml) and 2 tsp (10 ml) coconut oil |

| The Recipe Calls For | Substitution |
|---|---|
| 1 cup (227 grams) of butter<br>= 2 sticks of butter<br>= 8 ounces<br>= 22 grams | ½ cup (119 ml) pureed or canned pumpkin plus ½ cup plus 2 tsp. (9.86 ml) coconut oil |
| | ½ cup (119 ml) pureed pears plus ½ cup plus 2 tsp. (9.86 ml) coconut oil |
| | ½ cup (119 ml) nonfat yogurt plus ½ cup plus 2 tsp. (9.86 ml) coconut oil |
| | ½ cup plain yogurt (119 ml) plus ½ cup plus 2 tsp. (9.86 ml) coconut oil |
| | ½ cup (119 ml) mashed bananas plus ½ cup plus 2 tsp. (9.86 ml) coconut oil |
| | ½ cup pureed dates (119 ml) plus ½ cup plus 2 tsp. (9.86 ml) coconut oil |
| | ¼ cup to ½ cup (59 to 119 ml) of mashed or pureed prunes, either soaked or cooked plus 2 to 3 tsp. (13 – 19.5 g) lecithin granules. |

| The Recipe Calls For | Substitution |
|---|---|
| 1 cup (227 grams) shortening | 2/3 cup (158 ml) oil vegetable or canola oil or coconut oil |
| | 1 cup (227 g) minus 2 Tbsp. (9.5 g) lard |
| | 1-1/8 cups (256 g) butter or margarine (decrease salt called for in recipe by 1/2 tsp./3 g) |
| 1 cup shortening, melted (237 ml) | 1 cup vegetable or canola oil (237 ml) (only if the recipe specifies "melted" shortening) |
| | 1 cup (237 ml) melted coconut oil |

# Butter Volume & Weight Equivalents

|  | Cup | Gram | Oz | Pound | Kg | Tbsp | Tsp |
|---|---|---|---|---|---|---|---|
| ¼ stick | 1/8 | 28.4 | 1 oz | 0.0625 | 0.028Kg | 2 | 6 |
| half stick | 1/4 | 56.7g | 2 oz | 0.125 lb | 0.057Kg | 4 | 12 |
| 2/3 stick | 1/3 | 75.7g | 2.67 oz | 0.167 lb | 0.076Kg | 5 tbsp + 1 tsp | 16 |
| ¾ stick | 3/8 | 85g | 3 oz | 0.1875 lb | 0.085Kg | 6 | 18 |
| stick | 1/2 | 113.4g | 4 oz | 0.25 lb | 0.113Kg | 8 | 24 |
| 1 stick + 3/8 stick | 5/8 | 141.8g | 5 oz | 0.3125 lb | 0.142Kg | 10 | 30 |
| 1 stick + 1/3 stick | 2/3 | 151.2g | 5.33 oz | 0.33 lb | 0.151Kg | 10 tbsp + 2 tsp | 32 |
| 1 stick + ½ stick | 3/4 | 170.1g | 6 oz | 0.375 lb | 0.170Kg | 12 | 36 |
| 1 stick + ¾ stick | 7/8 | 198.5g | 7 oz | 0.4375 lb | 0.199Kg | 14 | 42 |
| two sticks | 1 | 226.8g | 8 oz | 0.5 lb | 0.227Kg | 16 | 48 |
| tablespoon | 3/50 | 14.2g | 0.5 oz | 0.03 lb | 0.014Kg | 1 | 3 |
| teaspoon | 1/50 | 4.7g | 0.167 oz | 0.01 lb | 0.004Kg | 1/3 | 1 |

Other wonderful substitutes to reduce the fat and calories in your cupcakes include substituting 50% of the fat with 50% of non-frozen pureed fruits (and even vegetables) such as bananas, dates, apples, applesauce, apple butter, prunes, zucchini, carrots, pear, and pumpkin.

## How to Test Fats for Freshness

You should use your oil or butter by the "Best if Used by …" date on the package. You can also taste the fat you are using. An edible fat will oxidize with age and begin to smell bad and taste sour when it goes rancid.

## Healthy Oil Substitutions (and Reducing Fat)

There are a lot of options to replace fat in cupcake recipes with healthier options for a healthier result. You may notice in the fat substitution chart that coconut oil is a substitute. Coconut oil is an excellent substitute for baking cupcakes. It contributes to a nice mouth feel and a tender crumb, plus there is plenty of evidence that coconut oil may have beneficial health effects.

Other wonderful substitutes to reduce the fat and calories in your cupcakes include substituting 50% of the fat with 50% of non-frozen pureed fruits (and even vegetables) such as bananas, dates, apples, applesauce, apple butter, prunes, zucchini, carrots, pear, and pumpkin. Add a bit of liquid to help puree them. Milk, soymilk, almond milk, or rice milk with some natural fat are good choices. Some of my favorite cupcake creations have used a combination of 50% organic virgin coconut oil and 50% apple butter or pureed pumpkin to substitute for the fat in the recipe. For the best results keep a minimum of 2 Tbsp. (28.4 g) of fat per cup (120 g/4.23 ounces) of flour in your cupcake recipe. Your body needs some fat to function as designed, and most cupcake recipes do, too.

Keep in mind that it's often more pleasurable in the long run to indulge your taste buds with a single unforgettable cupcake than a dozen cupcakes that taste like a compromise. Sometimes a single indulgence in a cupcake that sends tingles to your toes will satisfy you far longer and cost fewer calories overall.

Keep in mind that it's often more pleasurable in the long run to indulge your taste buds with a single unforgettable cupcake than a dozen cupcakes that taste like a compromise.

*Chapter 10*

# Sugar Does More than Sweeten Cupcakes

Sugar does more for cupcakes than sweeten them. It also adds volume and texture, affects the color and tenderness, and acts as a preservative. Sugar reduces the amount of gluten formed in the flour by attracting moisture in the batter, producing tender, lighter cupcakes. As long as your cupcake recipe has 2 Tbsp. (25 grams) of sugar per cup (120 g/4.23 oz) of flour, the sugar will prevent the proteins in the flour from forming strong gluten chains and will bond with the sugar instead. Avoiding the formation of strong gluten chains is necessary to produce tender, light cupcakes.

The more sugar there is in a recipe, the darker brown the cupcake's crust will be. Sugar also caramelizes during the baking process, pumping up the yummy flavor. Less sugar results in a lighter cupcake crust and less caramelized flavor. The level of browning is the result of the amount of sugar interacting with the protein in the milk and eggs, combined with the heat of the oven.

The amount of and type of sugar or sugar substitute used also affects the volume, moisture and tenderness of the cupcake.

There are numerous types of sugars, and the type of sugar you choose determines how much air is incorporated

Sugar reduces the amount of gluten formed in the flour by attracting moisture in the batter, producing tender, lighter cupcakes.

Sugar also caramelizes during the baking process, pumping up the yummy flavor.

into the batter during creaming. Granulated sugar incorporates more air into the batter while confectioner's sugar dissolves more quickly. Cupcake recipes most often call for granulated sugar. Some bakers also use castor sugar, which dissolves quickly and gives cupcakes a light texture.

Sugar also caramelizes in baking, which enriches flavors. Substituting as little as one Tbsp. (15 ml) of corn syrup for sugar can make cookies much browner, because corn syrup browns at a lower temperature than sugar. Some sugars, like honey and brown sugar, absorb moisture from the atmosphere, which means that things baked with them will stay soft and moist longer. A sweetener that absorbs and draws in moisture to the cupcake is called hygroscopic.

### Sugar Substitutes

Substituting another sweetener for sugar involves changing the baking chemistry of your cupcake recipe. There are more choices than ever, although some are healthier than others.

Since the goal of all my baking is to create cupcakes that don't compromise on taste and can be customized with healthier substitutes, I use Stevia blends and agave nectar, two natural sweeteners generally regarded as safe substitutes for sugar for diabetics. Xylitol and powdered fructose are also natural sugar substitutes that look and taste like sugar that I have just started experimenting with.

Other natural choices include maple syrup, brown rice syrup, honey and blackstrap molasses. There are also manufactured substitutes such as Splenda a.k.a Sucralose.

### Agave as a Sweetener

Agave nectar, commonly referred to as just "agave," is a medium caramel-like flavored natural sweetener. Its syrupy consistency can be substituted for sugar by reducing the amount used in the recipe by 1/4 or 25%. This means you will use 3/4 of the amount of agave nectar to replace the sugar used in the recipe.

You also need to reduce the other liquids in the recipe by 1/3, or 33%. This substitution amount is not a hard and fast rule. You may want to play with the exact amount to retain the moisture and reduce the calories or sugar more. As with any cupcake experiment, the kind of cupcake recipe you are adapting will play a chemical role. Agave can substitute for honey on a 1:1 basis. When substituting agave for sugar, reduce the oven temperature by 25°F, 14°C.

### Stevia as a Sweetener

Stevia, short for Stevia rebaudiana, is a plant in the sunflower family grown for its sweet leaves in the tropics of Central and South America. Used for more than 200 years in native areas as a sweetener, it is available in concentrates of white powder and clear liquid. It adds zero calories in its pure form.

The Reb-A extract, also known as Rebaudioside A or Rebiana, is a natural sweetening agent extracted from the sweetest part of the Stevia leaves, and has been approved as a food additive in the United States since December 2008. Stevia itself is classified as a supplement. Cargill, in conjunction with the Coca-Cola Company, and Pure Circle, in conjunction with PepsiCo, have each developed a sweetener based on this Stevia extract.

Millions of Japanese have used Stevia over the past 30 years with no reported ill effects. Medical research has even shown there may be health benefits to using Stevia. This zero calories sweetener may be good news for people suffering from diabetes, obesity and high blood pressure. Since the Stevia leaf has a tendency to lower glucose levels, it is a great natural sweetener substitute, except for people with low blood sugar or hypoglycemia. The other forms of Stevia may or may not have this property.

Substituting Stevia for sugar in cupcakes and other baked goods is a bit challenging in reality unless you use a Stevia and sugar blend such as Sun Crystals® (discussed further in this section). To adjust your cupcake recipe for the use of Stevia, you can use ¼ cup (59 ml) of apple, pumpkin or pear puree (depending on the flavor you want) with the prescribed equivalent (varies by brand due to the presence or absence of other ingredients and fillers) of Stevia blend for each cup (201 g/7.1 oz) of sugar called for in the recipe. Pear puree has the mildest flavor and is one of the easiest natural fruit purees to use in place of sugar. With the addition of Stevia in the correct proportion, you can retain a similar level of sweetness. The addition of a couple of tablespoons (25 g) of sugar can help retain the natural browning and mouth feel if you are not opposed to a small amount of sugar in your recipe.

Now that a Stevia leaf extract is approved in the U.S. as a sweetener, it is available in concentrations that only include the sweetest part of the Stevia plant leaves and in blends with all natural ingredients. Stevia leaf extract is available under brand names Truvia (www.truvia.com), Purevia (www.purevia.com), and Zsweet (www.zsweet.com).

Purevia is certified Kosher Parve and is an all natural and non-genetically modified Stevia leaf extract blend. Substitute Purevia for sugar by using ¼ or 25% of the amount of Purevia as sugar called for in the recipe. Truvia is also kosher certified and you can substitute Truvia at ½ the amount of sugar called for in the recipe. Target also carries a sugar substitute with Stevia extract in their Market Pantry brand that also tastes excellent and substitutes for sugar at ½ cup Market Pantry Sugar Substitute to 1 cup sugar.

Another commercially available Stevia mix, blended especially for baking, is Sun Crystals® (www.suncrystals. com). This brand includes sugar. The mixture claims the same sweetening power as sugar with half the calories and carbohydrates. This blend would retain the browning property and mouth feel of sugar, yet reduces the blood glucose effects. The Sun Crystals website states the product is suitable for people with diabetes and provides

Now that a Stevia leaf extract is approved in the U.S. as a sweetener, it is available in concentrations that only include the sweetest part of the Stevia plant leaves and in blends with all natural ingredients.

This non-GMO brand is in manufactured in the United States from organic birch hardwood.

natural sweetness with fewer calories and carbohydrates. Up to 3 packets, or one tsp. (3.9 g) counts as a "free food" for diabetics.

Zsweet® (www.zsweet.com) is kosher, non-GMO (a non-genetically modified product), has zero calories and does not affect the blood sugar. The Zsweet website says that Zsweet is far superior in taste to Stevia and closer in taste to sugar. The website recommends substituting 50% of the sugar with Zsweet.

Sun Crystals® and Zsweet® are currently the only two Stevia extract blends available in a bag for baking. Purevia® and Truvia® are available in packets. You have to have to calculate the number of packets to use or tear open and shake into measuring tools.

### Xylitol as a Sugar Substitute

Xylitol is a natural sugar alcohol occurring in a variety of fruits, vegetables and hardwoods. This sweetener is considered safe for use by diabetics. All commercially available Xylitol is manufactured in China; most is derived from corn except for a brand called Smart Sweet® by Global Sweet. This non-GMO brand is manufactured in the United States from organic birch hardwood.

Substitute Xylitol on a one-to-one basis for sugar. In Finland, baked goods are often made using Xylitol or there is a Xylitol alternative. With 75% fewer carbs, 40% fewer calories, Xylitol, even in small amounts, may have some side effects that are more serious in some people than others.  These symptoms include gas, diarrhea, stomach discomfort, oral erosive eczema or even acute renal failure. Although generally tolerated by most people in moderate doses without any side effects, I myself am sensitive to Xylitol. However, my recent experiments substituting half the sugar with it in cupcakes have helped me from over indulging in the deliciousness of the cupcakes since I do not like the gastrointestinal effects I get when ingesting too much. I am automatically limited to one cupcake by using Xylitol.

**WARNING:** You should NEVER give your dog or any pet anything containing Xylitol as it is assimilated biologically differently by animals and results in seizures and death.

## Sugar Substitution Chart

| | Amount | Glycemic Index Value | Weight of 1 cup in Ounces | Weight 1 cup in Grams | Calories per serving equivalent | Browns/ Carmelizes | Hygroscopic |
|---|---|---|---|---|---|---|---|
| Table Sugar | 1 cup (201 grams) | 68 | 7.1 | 201 | 806 | Yes | Yes |
| Pasteurized Honey | 2/3 - ¾ cup (158 - 178 ml), reduce liquid by ¼ cup (59 ml), add ¼ tsp. (1 g) baking soda per cup honey. Reduce oven temperature by 25 degree. You may need to decrease baking time. | 58 – 83 (depends on brand) | 12 | 340 | 720 480 | Yes | Yes |
| Raw Honey | 2/3 - ¾ cup (158 - 178 ml), reduce liquid by ¼ cup 59 ml), add ¼ tsp. (1 g) baking soda per cup honey. Reduce oven temperature by 25°F, 14°C. You may need to decrease baking time. | 30 | 12 | 340 | 720 480 | Yes | Yes |
| Agave Nectar | 3/4 cup (178 ml) – less 1/3 other liquids and decrease oven temperature 25°F, 14°C. | 1.6 – 27 (depending on brand) | 12 | 340 | 240 - 320 | Yes | Yes |
| Stevia (Pure white powder form, not a blend) | ¼ tsp. (varies by brand) | 0 | varies by brand | varies by brand | 0 | No | No |
| Purevia® | 24 sticks of Purevia | 0 | 1.68 | 48 g | 0 | No | No |

| | Amount | Glycemic Index Value | Weight of 1 cup in Ounces | Weight 1 cup in Grams | Calories per serving equivalent | Browns/ Carmelizes | Hygroscopic |
|---|---|---|---|---|---|---|---|
| Truvia® | ½ cup | 0 | 2.96 | 84 g | 0 | No | No |
| Sun Crystals® (with Stevia Extract) | ½ cup | 92 | 1.1 | 31.2 g | 403 | Yes | Yes |
| Xylitol | 1 cup | 7 | 6.77 | 192 g | 0 | No | Slightly |
| Unsulfured Blackstrap Molasses | ½ to 3/4 cup (119 – 178 ml)^ | 55 | 12.42 | 352 g | 360 – 720 (depending on brand & amount used) | Yes | Yes |
| Date Sugar | 1 cup | 103 | 6.77 | 192 g | 720 | Yes | Yes |
| Brown Rice Syrup | 1-1/3 cup (458 g), decrease liquids by ¼ cup, add 1/4 tsp. (1 g) baking soda | 25 | 12.13 | 344 g | 904 | Yes | Yes |
| Barley Malt Syrup (not Barley/Corn Malt Syrup) | 1-1/3 cup (316 ml), reduce liquids by ¼ cup, add ¼ tsp. (1 g) baking soda per cup barley malt syrup | 42 | 11.85 | 336 g | 1276 | Yes | Yes |

| | Amount | Glycemic Index Value | Weight of 1 cup in Ounces | Weight 1 cup in Grams | Calories per serving equivalent | Browns/ Carmelizes | Hygroscopic |
|---|---|---|---|---|---|---|---|
| Maple Syrup | ¾ to 1-1/2 cup (178 – 355 ml), minus 2–4 Tbsp. (30 – 60 ml) liquid, Add ¼-½ tsp. (1 – 2 g) baking soda. Decrease oven temp by 25°F, 14°C. | 54 | 11.36 | 322 g | 624 - 1248 | Yes | Yes |
| Maple Sugar | 1 cup plus 1/8 tsp. (.75 g) baking soda per cup | 68 | 5.08 | 144 g | 720 | Yes | Yes |
| Turbinado Sugar | 1 cup | 65 | 6.77 | 192 g | 576 | Yes | Yes |
| Fructose (Granulated) | ½ cup | 17 | 6.91 | 196 g | 721 | Yes | Yes |
| Splenda® Sugar Blend | 1/2 cup | 65 | 6.77 | 192 g | 768 | No | No |

*Measured in liquid equivalents

*Chapter 11*

# Eggs

Eggs are an important ingredient. Their purpose is to bind the ingredients, leaven (expand) the batter and lighten the crumb of the cupcake. The egg white and egg yolk can be used in the cupcake recipe in different ways.

The egg yolk is considered nature's great emulsifier, allowing the butter and other fats in the recipe to remain combined, almost permanently suspended, in the water-based ingredients of the cupcake batter. The egg yolk also adds creaminess to the batter texture. If you prefer to use egg whites only in your batter, you can keep the creamy emulsifying effect of whole eggs in your cupcake batter by adding two teaspoons (10 ml) of soy lecithin. You can melt the soy lecithin with a couple tablespoons of hot water and decrease the amount of other liquid by the same amount to use it in your cupcake recipes. Bob's Red Mill has excellent soy lecithin.

You can also substitute shortening for butter since shortening contains emulsifiers. If you are making a recipe with strong flavor such as chocolate, many bakers find success substituting olive oil for the fat in the recipe since olive oil also contains natural emulsifiers (check the conversion table for the correct amount). Since olive oil has a strong taste, it does not translate well for most taste buds into a more delicately flavored cupcake like vanilla.

If you prefer to use egg whites only in your batter, you can keep the creamy emulsifying effect of whole eggs in your cupcake batter by adding two teaspoons (10 ml) of soy lecithin.

You can test the freshness of an egg by either shaking it or putting it in cold water. When shaken, a spoiled egg sloshes around; a fresh egg makes no sound. A fresh egg placed in cold water won't float; a bad egg will.

Whole eggs have a greater thickening power than either whites or yolks alone. The egg whites are a liquid protein and act as a binder and thickener in cupcake recipes. Egg whites substituted for whole eggs can dry out the crumb of the cupcake so you may want to add one teaspoon (5 ml) of oil per egg called for in the recipe or increase the liquid by 1 – 2 teaspoons (5 – 10 ml) per egg depending on the recipe. You cannot add oil to an egg foam or sponge cake type recipe, since this may ruin it.

Eggs should always be cracked into a clean container and never directly into the batter to avoid rotten eggs or pieces of shell from contaminating the mixture. Make sure the eggs are fresh before using them.

### How to Test Your Eggs for Freshness

You can test the freshness of an egg by either shaking it or putting it in cold water. When shaken, a spoiled egg sloshes around; a fresh egg makes no sound. A fresh egg placed in cold water won't float; a bad egg will.

You can also look at the insides of the egg. The whites of fresh eggs are opalescent or slightly cloudy and thick. The whites of older eggs are clear and thin. Regardless of the expiration date on the outside, if a cracked egg or even a whole egg has a runny yolk, red speckles inside, or smells bad, it is no good, and should be discarded.

### How to Separate Eggs

Room temperature eggs are harder to separate than cold eggs, so if you need egg whites only separate them right after taking them out of the refrigerator.

Crack the egg on an edge. Position the egg over a small clean bowl in the same position they are held in the egg container and gently pull off the top part of the eggshell. Pass the egg yolk back and forth between the two pieces of eggshells, allowing the egg whites to fall into the bowl below.

Put the yolks into a separate bowl. You can safely keep egg yolks in a covered container in the refrigerator for 3 days. You can also mix a pinch of salt or sugar with the egg yolks and pour the mixture into ice tray sections. Cover tightly with freezer wrap and store in the freezer for up to four months. If you skip the salt or sugar mixed with the yolks to act as a preservative, the yolks will be unusable later because the freezer turns them gelatinous.

Keep in mind that if you are using the egg whites in an egg foam or sponge cake mixture you need to avoid any oil getting in the mix. If a bit of yolk escapes into the egg whites, fish it out carefully with a spoon. Don't use an eggshell half to scoop it out, as the outside of the egg could be contaminated. Definitely don't fish it out with your finger since even the amount of oil on your fingertips will keep the egg whites from expanding.

If a recipe calls for egg whites only, separate the egg white from the yolk using an egg separator. Using an egg separator is better than cracking eggs by hand and passing

Room temperature eggs are harder to separate than cold eggs, so if you need egg whites only separate them right after taking them out of the refrigerator.

Put the yolks into a separate bowl. You can safely keep egg yolks in a covered container in the refrigerator for 3 days.

the yolk back and forth between the eggshells because it lessens the risk of exposing the egg to potentially harmful bacteria on the shell.

### Egg Whites in Cupcake Recipes

Egg whites are great for cupcakes because they trap air bubbles when beaten, serve as a binder and thickener, and make the batter lighter and fluffier. When using a recipe calling for egg whites, the cupcakes must be baked shortly after the egg whites are whipped. Egg whites start losing their water content and deflating after 5-6 minutes and cannot be rewhipped to their original volume and stability.

### Whole Eggs in Cupcake Recipes

Many cupcake recipes call for whole eggs. Whole eggs are used in recipes that require creaming and create a moist, stable batter. Room temperature eggs should be added to the batter one at a time, and usually after the shortening or butter and the sugar have been creamed. If eggs are added too quickly, the mixture can curdle, causing the sugar and fat to separate.

If you find yourself out of eggs, or you would like to substitute them for any reason, this chart will come in handy.

When using a recipe calling for egg whites, the cupcakes must be baked shortly after the egg whites are whipped.

## Egg Substitution Chart

| Substitute for 1 egg | Equivalency to 1 egg |
| --- | --- |
| Egg Yolks | 2 egg yolks |
| Egg Whites | 2 egg whites, plus 1 - 2 teaspoons (5 – 10 ml) liquid<br>or oil per egg amount in the recipe |
| Frozen Eggs (thawed) | 3 Tbsp. (45 ml) plus 1 tsp. (5 ml)<br>thawed frozen egg |
| Liquid Refrigerated Egg Product | Per carton instructions |
| Powdered Eggs | 2 Tbsp. and<br>2 tsp. dry (12 g) whole egg powder<br>plus an equal amount of water |
| Flaxmeal | 1 Tbsp. (6 g) Flaxmeal Plus<br>2 Tbsp. (30 ml) hot water. Let stand<br>10 min. until gooey. |
| Lecithin Powder | 1 Tbsp. (8 g) lecithin powder minus 1 Tbsp. fat (14 g) from recipe, plus add 2 Tbsp. (30 ml) liquid |
| Soft Silken Tofu | 1/4 cup (59 ml) soft silken tofu<br>blended with liquids in the recipe |
| Soy Yogurt | 1/4 cup (59 ml) soy yogurt, minus<br>1 Tbsp. (15 ml) liquid in the recipe |

| | |
|---|---|
| Bananas | ½ banana mashed up (works in heavier textured products using muffin or quick bread type recipes) |
| Applesauce | ¼ cup (59 ml) of applesauce (works in heavier textured products using muffin or quick bread type recipes) |

### Eggs as a Partial Sugar Substitute

You may also up the number of eggs (binding agents) by 25 – 50%. You can also add a tsp. (5 ml) of ground flaxseed with a tsp. (5 ml) or two of water instead of increasing the number of eggs.

Of course, these are general guidelines. The substitution for each recipe depends on the other ingredients in the recipe and whether you are at or high above sea level. Altitude matters in baking. For example, you need to reduce the oven 25°F, 14°C for the agave substitution at sea level but increase the oven 25°F, 14°C if you bake at high altitude. So, if you substitute agave for sugar in a high altitude recipe and you change nothing else, then the oven temperature can remain the same. Look Ma, no hands!

On the next page is a chart of sugar substitutes for your cupcake baking adventures!

If you substitute agave for sugar in a high altitude recipe and you change nothing else, then the oven temperature can remain the same.

*Chapter 12*

# Cupcake Mix-Ins

Mix-ins are candies, fruit, sprinkles, nuts, or marshmallows that can be added to the cake batter to give the cupcakes extra texture and favorite flavors. Mix-ins should be added after the batter has been thoroughly mixed and just before pouring it into the muffin tins. This is an easy and creative way to add a custom touch to a basic cupcake recipe.

When the batter has just been mixed, it's time to fill the cupcake tin. There are many effective methods for filling the cups in the muffin tin. You can use a decorating bag, a sandwich bag, an ice cream scoop, a ladle, a spoon, or a measuring cup. Whichever method you use, gather the required supplies before you start mixing up the batter. For the lightest fluffiest cupcakes, you don't want to keep your cupcakes waiting too long for the oven while you search for that bag of mini M&Ms you bought but can't seem to find when you need them.

Mix-ins should be added after the batter has been thoroughly mixed and just before pouring it into the muffin tins.

*Chapter 13*

# What Ingredients Do in Your Cupcake Recipes

The main components of cupcake recipes are structure, tenderizers, moisteners and leaveners. Flour and eggs are the main components for structure. Sugar and fat for tenderness. The following charts give you an overview of ingredients by their functions in the recipe. In the Advanced Cupcaking Section you can discover how to create cupcake recipes from scratch using the base formulas you need to formulate your own cupcake recipes.

The main components of cupcake recipes are structure, tenderizers, moisteners and leaveners. Flour and eggs are the main components for structure. Sugar and fat for tenderness.

## By Function

| | |
|---|---|
| Flavors (avoid artificial flavors) | Vanilla, Sugar, Salt, Butter, Chocolate, Cocoa, Flavor Extracts |
| Moisteners | Water, Syrups, Agave, Honey (other liquid sweeteners), Milk (liquids and liquid substitutes) |
| Tenderizers (weakens structure so cupcakes are not tough) | Egg yolks, Emulsifiers, Fats, Sugar, Leaveners, Gums, and Starches |
| Structure and Strengtheners | Flour, Eggs, Egg White, Gums, Milk Solids, Leaveners |
| Leaveners | Air beaten into the batter, Creaming Butter and Sugar together, Creaming Eggs and Butter together, Beaten Egg Whites (Meringue), Eggs beaten to the color lemon, Liquid in batter turns to steam created during baking, Baking Powder, Baking Soda, Cream of Tartar, Agar |

## By Ingredient

| | |
|---|---|
| Flour | Provides bulk/volume and structure. |
| Sugar, natural syrups, honey and agave nectar | Flavor, sweetness, fine texture, tenderness, caramelizing/browning of the crust; combined with fat, sugars act as a creaming agent; combined with eggs, sugars incorporate air bubbles into the mixture. |
| Egg yolks | Emulsifies, smoothes the batter, traps air bubbles, which adds to the volume, adds moisture and flavor, improves nutritional value, improves color and softens the texture. |
| Egg whites | Provides structure, traps air bubbles, adds moisture and nutritional value, helps improve color. |

| | |
|---|---|
| **Leaveners**<br><br>• Air beaten into the batter<br>• Creaming Butter and Sugar together<br>• Creaming Eggs and Butter together<br>• Beaten Egg Whites (meringue), Eggs beaten to the color lemon<br>• Liquid in batter turns to steam created during baking<br>• Baking Powder<br>• Baking Soda<br>• Cream of Tartar<br>• Agar Agar | Incorporates and expands air bubbles in the mixture that rise during the baking process and are fixed in place by the oven. |
| **Fat**<br><br>• Butter<br>• Oils<br>• Lard<br>• Egg Yolks | Softens, tenderizes, adds flavor, moistness, and assists the leaveners. |
| **Fresh Fruit** | Adds sweetness, flavor and nutrition. |

| | |
|---|---|
| Dried Fruit | Adds flavor, sweetness and nutrition. Soak them in water or juice and dry with a paper towel before adding them to batter or they will compete with the batter for moisture. |
| Frozen Fruit | Adds flavor, sweetness and nutrition. Warm to room temperature, and if thawed and is liquidy, then reduce liquids by ½ to ¾ of the amount of fruit. |
| Gums<br>• Agar (Marine Plant)<br>• Xanthan (Microbial Polysaccharide)<br>• Pectin (Terrestrial Plant) | Thickeners and stabilizers. Can prevent liquids from seeping out of gels. Used mainly in gum paste and certain kinds of icing to prevent stickiness and cracking. |

When analyzing or designing cupcake recipes, be sure the ingredients that tenderize do not overpower the ingredients that create the cake's structure. When this imbalance of ingredients happens, the cake will fall or fail to rise very high before it sets in the oven. Too many fats and sugars not balanced with enough flour and leaveners result in compact, poor volume cupcakes. Too much flour and leaveners without enough fats or sugar result in dense, chewy cupcakes.

*Chapter 14*

# The Right Temperature for Ingredients

Ingredients such as eggs and butter should be allowed to warm at least to room temperature before being mixed into the batter. A temperature warmer than room temperature is even better, except for butter.

Do not melt butter to hurry the process, because this will affect the quality and consistency of the batter, unless the recipe calls for melted fat.

Do not melt butter to hurry the process, because this will affect the quality and consistency of the batter, unless the recipe calls for melted fat.

### No Time? How to Warm Ingredients to Room Temperature
### How to Warm Eggs

If you add cold eggs into the mix they harden the fat (butter or oil) in the recipe, curdling the sugar and fat mixture and affecting the texture of the cupcakes. Mixing cold items with room temperature batter may lead to lumpy batter, over mixing and flat cupcakes.

Place your eggs in a medium bowl. Run the tap water to hot and fill the bowl 3/4 full to cover the eggs. Let the eggs sit for 6-9 minutes and remove the eggs with a large spoon. The eggs will not cook and will be warm. Eggs that are at room temperature or warmer beat to a greater volume.

If you already cracked open your eggs and need them warmed up quick, fill the sink 1/3 with hot water and place your bowl of eggs in the water for 5 minutes. Presto, warm eggs!

### How to Warm Butter

There are several ways to warm butter without melting it.
- Let sit out at room temperature for 1 - 2 hours.
- Cut the butter into small slices into your stand mixer and mix until soft.
- Cut butter into ¼ cup (59 g) or ½ stick amounts and put in the microwave for 10 seconds at a time in 8 - 10 seconds bursts for each ¼ cup (59 g) of butter.
- Dice the butter into ½ inch by ½ inch, 12.7 mm by 12.7 mm cubes and set out for 20 minutes at room temperature.

**How to Warm Milk or Other Liquid**

Warm liquid to the perfect temperature in a heatproof glass measuring cup by microwaving on high for 25-35 seconds. This will warm milk up to body temperature, perfect for cupcake batter.

Part 3

# The Perfect
## *Batter*

*Chapter 15*

# Preparing the Batter for Unforgettable Cupcakes

Now that quality ingredients have been gathered, it is time to create cupcake batter. The steps of the recipe must be followed carefully because accidentally skipping a step can lead to lousy results. Once you get the knack of mixing ingredients for cupcakes, you may start to feel like the rules don't apply to you anymore. I once had those thoughts. What a mess, what a waste. I want to cry remembering the "almost born" key lime cupcakes. The rules of cupcake science always apply in your kitchen, no matter how long you bake those cupcakes.

> The rules of cupcake science always apply in your kitchen, no matter how long you bake those cupcakes.

### Methods of Mixing for Unforgettable Cupcakes

It matters which method you use. When you make traditional cupcakes with flour, the final texture is influenced by the amount of gluten content and by how you mix the recipe. The higher the gluten percentage of the flour you use, the denser the structure. The longer you mix the batter, the denser the cupcake.

> When you make traditional cupcakes with flour, the final texture is influenced by the amount of gluten content, and by how you mix the recipe.

You want to avoid overmixing cupcake batter because the gluten strands formed in the batter by mixing the

Salt in a cupcake recipe heightens the sweetening power of the sugar in the recipe and allows you to use less sugar.

flour with liquid ingredients grow stronger the more you mix. The stronger the gluten strands, the less the strands allow the air bubbles trapped to expand and the tougher the cupcake texture.

Here are some of the reasons you want to know how to mix various kinds of cupcake recipes:

- So you can invent your own cupcake recipes
- So you can understand how changing a recipe may affect how you mix the ingredients for successful results based on your changes
- So you can check to be sure the recipe you are using for the first time includes the correct mixing instructions for the best outcome (not all recipes are created by bakers who know these secrets)
- So you can just plain impress yourself!

On to the methods for mixing unforgettable cupcakes…

### General Guidelines for Mixing Cupcake Batter

These guidelines apply to mixing cupcakes.

- When baking powder is used as leavening with a type of wheat flour (includes all-purpose, cake, pastry and wheat pastry flours) the amount of mixing is limited. Overmixing will strengthen the gluten chains and toughen the texture.
- Salt in a cupcake recipe heightens the sweetening power of the sugar in the recipe and allows you to use less sugar. It should not be eliminated, as the

small amount of salt in a cupcake recipe will not harm you. Of course, if you have health issues you should always check with your doctor first, as I am a Cupcake Chef, not a doctor, of course.

- The ratio of fat and sugar to flour is the key to the variances in the method you use to mix the batter. You can mix a cupcake recipe higher in fat and sugar for a longer time with less toughening of the texture. Cupcake recipes proportionally lower in fat and sugar are mixed for a much shorter period and have a more muffin-like or bread-like texture.

- Sugar is considered a wet ingredient in the baking world.

You can mix a cupcake recipe higher in fat and sugar for a longer time with less toughening of the texture.

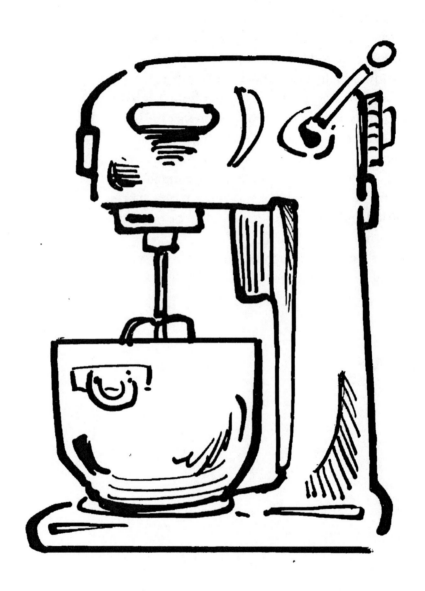

*Chapter 16*

# How to Choose the Mixing Method for Cupcake Recipes

When you adapt a cupcake or muffin recipe or create a recipe from scratch, the mixing method you choose is a major factor in creating taste bud tempting cupcakes. The method you choose to mix will affect the final product. If you tweak a recipe to reduce or replace the fat and sugar or check the recipe you are using to ensure that it recommends the correct mixing method, it's important to calculate the amount of sugar and butter in ratio to the amount of flour.

As covered in the previous section, the ratio of fat and sugar to flour determines the method for mixing you use.

If Sugar Weight + Fat Weight > = Flour Weight, then use the Creaming Method.

If Sugar Weight + Fat Weight < = Flour Weight, then use the Muffin Method.

Eggs with No fat = Egg Foam Method

When you adapt a cupcake or muffin recipe or create a recipe from scratch, the mixing method you choose is a major factor in creating taste bud tempting cupcakes.

### The Muffin Method

Also known as the two-bowl method, this mixing method uses the least amount of mixing. This method is used for muffin based cupcake recipes. These typically contain a ratio of less than ½ fat and sugar to flour and are based on the American style of muffins, which use a chemical leavener such as baking soda or baking powder. English muffin recipes use yeast and fall into the bread category.

American-style muffins can be further divided into two categories:

1. cake-like
2. bread-like

The difference between the two types is in the amount of fat and butter. The less butter and sugar, the more bread-like the texture. The more butter and sugar, the more cake-like the texture. The type of fat also varies. Bread-like muffin recipes usually use a liquid fat, like melted butter or vegetable oil.

Many muffin recipes fall somewhere in the middle of the spectrum between a cake-like or bread-like texture. Cupcake recipes such as pumpkin cupcakes may be based on a pumpkin muffin recipe. When you decrease the fat and sugar in a cupcake recipe, your cupcake's texture will naturally become more bread-like. This knowledge will help you choose the type of cupcake texture you prefer, and choose or adapt recipes to match your preferred texture.

When you decrease the fat and sugar in a cupcake recipe, your cupcake's texture will naturally become more bread-like.

If you want your cupcakes to have a muffin-like texture or you are reducing the fat and sugar in your recipe below the ½ fat and sugar to flour ratio, this is the method to use. With the Muffin Method, you prepare the batter so as not to develop the gluten resulting in a batter texture with larger, uneven air bubbles. The desired result using a muffin type recipe is a symmetrical cupcake with a nicely browned, domed top that has doubled in volume. The surface will also be bumpy, the texture tender and moist and the cupcake will feel light for its size.

Blend the dry ingredients in one bowl and the liquid ingredients in another bowl. The ingredients are combined just until the flour mixture is absorbed in the liquid mixture, resulting in a lumpy, not smooth batter. Overmixing this type of batter prevents it from rising in the early part of the baking cycle. Keep in mind, the lower the fat content in your cupcake recipe, the less mixing you want to do after adding the flour.

Keep in mind, the lower the fat content in your cupcake recipe, the less mixing you want to do after adding the flour.

Keys to the Muffin Method include:
- Begin and end with the dry ingredients. Sift the dry ingredients together. Mix the liquid ingredients, adding the separately well-beaten eggs last to the liquids. Add the bowl of wet ingredients to the bowl of dry ingredients until moistened.
- Use a wooden spoon, turning the mixture slowly, as little as possible, about 45 seconds only, until the large pockets of flour have disappeared and the mixture is moistened.

- Add in ingredients such as chocolate chips or blueberries by folding in after the flour is moistened, only until you have evenly distributed them in the batter.

### The Creaming Method

The Creaming Method, also known as the sugar batter or sugar shortening method, and the conventional method, is used for the richest cakes. This method is used for rich cupcake mixtures where there is a more than ½ fat and sugar to flour ratio.

Begin by beating the butter and sugar together. Beating is the process of using an electric mixer to load up as many tiny air bubbles as possible, so your cupcakes will be light and tender and rise in the oven.

Cream the butter and sugar together in a large bowl. The types of sugar used in the creaming method typically are white granular sugar (also known as table sugar), superfine sugar (table sugar ground into finer granules), or brown sugar. The length of time spent creaming determines the amount of air in the batter; the fluffier the butter-sugar mixture, the lighter the cupcakes will be.

Creaming is very important and should take 8-10 minutes. Start on a low speed when using an electric mixer, then increase the speed and periodically scrape the sides of the bowl to make sure all the sugar gets mixed in. Sugar that has not been properly beaten into the batter can make for heavier cupcakes with fine white specks on their tops.

The Creaming Method is used for rich cupcake mixtures where there is a more than ½ fat and sugar to flour ratio.

Stop beating the mixture when it is a very pale yellow in color and fluffy. Don't overcream or cream too fast, because it will make the fat break down and release the previously creamed air bubbles. When creamed properly, the batter will be light and fluffy, and you will not be able to see the sugar grains because the butter and sugar have combined.

Add one egg at a time, mixing thoroughly and on low speed so the batter doesn't curdle. Another option when it comes to eggs is to separate the yolk from the egg whites and mix them separately. First beat the yolk until creamy and then add it to the butter/ sugar mixture. Next, beat the egg whites until they are frothy and add them by folding them in as the last step. Some bakers believe this makes for better cake batter. I do!

Wet ingredients should be combined in a separate bowl and then added to the creamed mixture. Next, combine the dry ingredients in a fresh bowl and gently and slowly add it to the creamed batter. Mix until just blended, because overmixing leads to dry, chewy and coarse cupcakes.

### The Rubbing-In Method

Also known as the Push-in Method, this is great for cupcake recipes that are low in fat or sugar. Start by sifting the flour and baking powder into a mixing bowl. Press the fat in the recipe (butter or shortening) into the flour until the mixture looks like tiny crumbs. Blend in the sugar and liquid. The blended mixture will be smooth, thick, and free from any lumps.

Next, beat the egg whites until they are frothy and add them by folding them in as the last step.

To achieve the optimal volume, let the egg whites sit out at room temperature for 30 minutes, and beat on the medium-high setting on your mixer.

The sugar whipped with the egg whites in egg-based cupcake recipes melts into the eggs as they are beaten.

### The Egg Foam Method

Also known as the whipping or whisking method, these egg foam or sponge cake type recipes are created by whipping air into the elastic structure of liquid egg whites. Egg whites contain a protein, which is developed by whipping or beating them, whether by hand, hand mixer or stand mixer. Much as you fill a balloon with air, egg foam is a giant mob of tiny egg balloons that hold up your sponge type cake recipes. Egg whites right out of the refrigerator will not hold much air. To achieve the optimal volume, let the egg whites sit out at room temperature for 30 minutes, and beat on the medium-high setting on your mixer.

When whipping egg whites, it is important that not one bit of oil is in the mixture. Not even a tiny bit of yolk; this is the fat in the egg. Make certain all the utensils and the bowl you use are free from fat or oil, including oils from your fingertips.

Fat retards the volume of the eggs you whip. You can still whip eggs with their yolks; they just do not whip up to the volume that egg yolks free of fat do.

The best kinds of bowls to whip egg whites are glass, stainless steel and copper. Plastic bowls can retain oils, which will keep the egg whites from expanding to their full potential.

The sugar whipped with the egg whites in egg-based cupcake recipes melts into the eggs as they are beaten. Sugar stiffens and sweetens the foam, dissolving into the egg white proteins. In sponge or egg type cakes, the sugar content is high and fixes the structure of the egg foam as it is heated in the oven.

Some recipes use whipped whole eggs and even just the yolks. If a recipe calls for both whipped yolks and whipped egg whites, whip the yolks first. You want to always whip egg whites as close as possible to the time when you add them into the batter.

### Steps for the Egg Foam Method

1.  Whisk, and then sift the dry ingredients together.
2.  Whip the eggs called for in the recipe with the sugar in a large bowl until the mixture is tripled in volume, light in color, and creamy.
3.  Sift the dry ingredients into the egg/sugar mixture and fold the combination together carefully.

### The Melted Method

As the name implies, the fat for the cupcake recipe is melted. Cupcakes mixed under the melted method usually contain a greater amount of sugar. Rather than a single method, the Melted Method includes two different methods: the Combination Melted Method for lighter cupcake recipes, and the Blending Melted Method for heavier, more compact cupcake recipes.

## Other Methods

**The Combination Melted Method** is a method used to lighten a dense cake recipe. The fat used in the recipe is either melted shortening or melted butter or oil.

1. Sift the flour. Chemical leaveners are usually not used in this method. However, if you do use either baking soda or baking powder, mix and sift it in with the flour at this step.
2. Cream together the fat and the flour with a paddle until soft. Whip the sugar and eggs together as in the egg foam method. Add the flavoring and add-in ingredients.
3. Fold the sugar/egg mixture into the fat/flour mixture.

**The Blended Melted Method** is used for a cupcake recipe with a higher amount of liquids and sugar, creating a moist, dense, tender crumb. The fat in the recipe coats the flour, inhibiting the formation of gluten. This mixing method creates a delicious texture; however, the volume will not be as high as the combination method above.

1. Mix and sift the flour and other dry ingredients together.
2. Add the oil, melted fat and a little liquid.
3. Beat thoroughly.
4. Add the eggs, flavoring and the remaining liquid.
5. Finish combining.

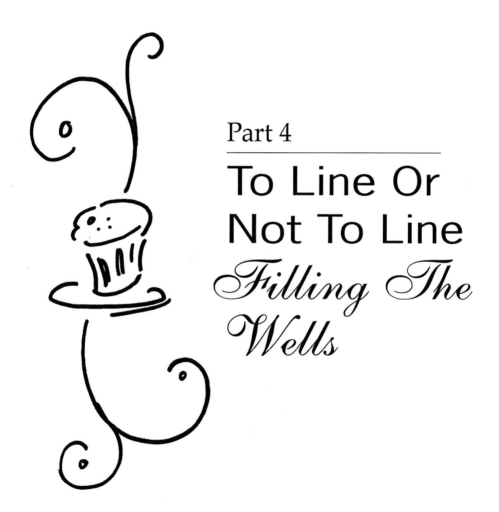

Part 4

## To Line Or Not To Line

### Filling The Wells

*Chapter 17*

# Introducing Cupcake Liners

Traditional cupcake liners are the papers that hug the bottom of the cupcakes. You need to peel away the liner to eat the whole cupcake. Cupcake liners sit in the cupcake or muffin tin wells and hold the batter.

There is a variety of cupcake liners available: from the reusable Silicone liners you can bake in, all the way to foil, wax coated paper, plain paper, parchment paper and biodegradable liners. There are also Japanese food liners (Bento), which are not made specifically as cupcake liners but are beautiful scalloped finishing elements that you can also bake directly in.

### The Sweet

To use or not to use cupcakes liners seems like a silly question. You might be surprised to learn it is one of the biggest questions many cupcake bakers face. Why? Cupcake liners affect the aesthetics of the presentation and the liner will change depending on the event you are making your cupcakes for. There are several factors to consider.

Cupcake liners protect cupcakes from drying out. Then, when you seal off the top of the cupcake from

You might be surprised to learn it is one of the biggest questions many cupcake bakers face.

Then, when you seal off the top of the cupcake from the air with a layer of frosting that meets the edge of the cupcake liner, the combination of the frosting and the liner preserve the freshness of the cupcake longer than a cupcake whose crumb is open to the air.

Some cupcake pundits have identified the cupcake liner problems as the "elephant in the cupcake room."

the air with a layer of frosting that meets the edge of the cupcake liner, the combination of the frosting and the liner preserve the freshness of the cupcake longer than a cupcake whose crumb is open to the air.

Since cupcakes are high in moisture, they are quick to go stale. Any method you can employ to protect the moist cupcake crumb from the air will extend its freshness. A liner allows you to make cupcakes ahead of time, to ship them, or to eat a whole batch yourself over a period of several days while they remain moist and yummy tasting.

Whenever you are baking cupcakes for bake sales, birthday parties, or any event where the cupcakes are passed from one person to another, you will want to use cupcake liners for sanitary reasons.

**The Sour**

Cupcake liners are sometimes cause for angst. Cupcakes, for seemingly mysterious reasons, stick to the liners, causing the cupcakes to peel off in chunks of cake along with the liner. The opposite problem is just as frustrating: The liner peels away from the cupcakes for no apparent reason.

Some cupcake pundits have identified the cupcake liner problems as the "elephant in the cupcake room." There are a lot of schools of thought about how to prepare and use cupcake liners to avoid these two opposite problems.

First, since baking is a delicious form of chemistry, if your recipe is correctly prepared and all the steps of baking are correctly followed, you may never run across cupcake liner problems. In fact, you may not run into any baking problems. However, a slight deviation could change all that.

### The Solution to Cupcake Liner Problems

Due to the variety of ingredients in recipes, some cupcake concoctions will react chemically with certain liners, with a variety of outcomes.  For example, metallic liners may add a slight metallic taste to certain cupcakes. Wax liners may separate more easily.

As a result of the various issues that can arise between the batter and the liner, some bakers swear by the ritual of spraying the inside of the liners prior to filling them with batter. Others find this increases the odds that the cupcake will separate or pull away from the liner before and even after the cupcakes have cooled down. The type of liner you use can also be a factor. Some newer paper liners have a waxy type coating more susceptible to premature separation.

If you have followed the recipe exactly, there could be many reasons your cupcakes stick to or separate from the cupcake liners. So is there a perfect solution? If you want to eliminate the possibility that you will have any cupcake liner issues, there are some steps you can take that will almost entirely eliminate the possibility of your cupcake liners sticking to or separating from the cupcakes.

If you have followed the recipe exactly, there could be many reasons your cupcakes stick to or separate from the cupcake liners.

*Chapter 18*

# Solving Cupcake Liner Problems

### Cupcake Liner Separation Issue Solution

- Use non-coated, plain paper cupcake liners.
- Fill the cupcake liners halfway.
- Do not spray them.
- While the cupcake tin is still in the oven, turn it around 180 degrees halfway through the baking time (at the 10 to 12-minute mark if the recipe calls for 20 minutes of baking time).
- Remove the cupcakes from the pan between the 3 to 5 minute mark after removing the pan from the oven.
- The most important step is to reduce condensation between the cupcakes and the paper by taking them out of the cupcake tin within the first 3 minutes they are out of the oven. This step will minimize the possibility that your cupcakes will be over baked; and when you remove them from the cupcake tin, you prevent steam from forming between the cupcake and the cupcake liner.

Paper and metallic cupcake liners can stick to the cupcakes like super glue for the first 24 hours after baking them. This sticking results in cupcakes that separate in chunks from the liners.

## Cupcake Liner Sticking Issue Solution

Paper and metallic cupcake liners can stick to the cupcakes like super glue for the first 24 hours after baking them. This sticking results in cupcakes that separate in chunks from the liners.

If you need to bake the cupcakes for a same-day event, you can use a baking flour spray. If you are baking gluten-free, then you can use a gluten-free baking spray and dust the inside of the cups with powdered sugar.

If you have the cupcake liner separation issue discussed above, then you can always set all the baked cupcakes into those colorful Silicone cupcake baking cups or the scalloped and decorative Bentos. You can even cut parchment squares (5 inches x 5 inches for a standard cupcake) and form each square around a cup bottom the size of the bottom of your cupcakes, set the cupcakes in those, and tie with a pretty ribbon or colorful yarn.

If you are making your cupcakes a day ahead of time, you will find the cupcake liners separate perfectly the next day, unless you have overbaked the cupcakes.

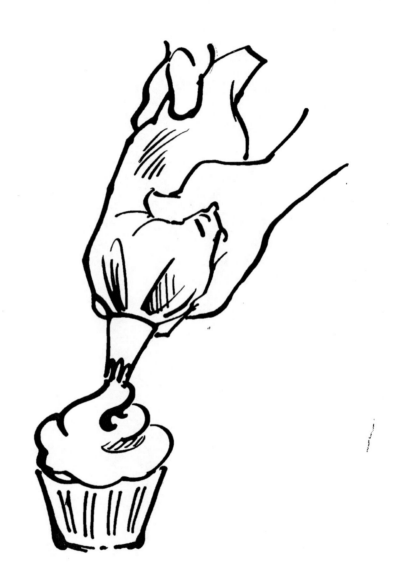

*Chapter 19*

# Filling the Cupcake Wells

A decorating bag is a very effective way to pour just the right amount of batter into each cup without spills. Fill the bag halfway with batter and simply squeeze controlled amounts of batter into the cups.

I frequently use a gallon size Ziploc bag. I set aside a clean medium sized bowl and line it with the gallon size bag as you would a garbage bag in a garbage can. Then I use a spatula to transfer the cupcake batter into the bag. I seal the bag and then snip a dime size hole in one of the bottom corners right above the first cupcake well. Then I gently squeeze just the right amount of batter into each cupcake well. This way I'm able to squeeze the batter into the cupcake liners without getting batter between the liner and the paper. Less mess, less stress.

You can throw the bag away when empty, rinse and recycle, or wash and reuse next time you make cupcakes! This is one of my favorite methods to fill cupcake wells because even I can keep the batter away from places it doesn't belong. I make a mess otherwise.

You can also use an ice cream or cookie dough scoop, a large spoon, a small ladle, a turkey baster or measuring cup to scoop batter from the mixing bowl and carefully

A decorating bag is a very effective way to pour just the right amount of batter into each cup without spills.

Underfilling leads to tiny, unimpressive cupcakes that bake too quickly.

pour or squeeze the batter into the cupcake wells. The ice cream or cookie dough scoop with a trigger or quick release is quick and easy (if you are not messy like me). Bakers everywhere call this method their favorite. For regular sized cupcakes look for a 56 – 59 ml or 2 ounce scoop. No matter what size scoop is used, make sure to fill the cup until it is 1/2 to 2/3 full.

I think it is really fun to use the turkey baster. Squeeze the big bulb at the top and stick it in the batter. Then release the bulb to suck the batter in. When I'm in a rush and not baking a thick battered cupcake, the turkey baster is a blast to use to fill the cupcake wells. It sounds fun and funny, right? It is!

The amount of batter per cupcake well depends on the pan size. Standard muffin cups require 1/3 to 1/2 cups (79 – 119 ml) of batter; mini cupcake pans take approximately 1 Tbsp. (15 ml). King-sized cupcake tins need just under a cup (237 ml) of batter, while jumbo cupcake pans require 1/2 to 2/3 cup (119 – 158 ml), and mini fancy-fill pans require ½ cup (119 ml) per pan. Overfilling can lead to messes and longer cooking times. Underfilling leads to tiny, unimpressive cupcakes that bake too quickly. A tray of cupcakes should be filled uniformly so that the cakes will bake in the same amount of time.

Before placing the pan in the oven, settle the batter by lightly shaking the pan. This helps the cupcakes bake more evenly. Do not tap your cupcake pan on the counter or you will destroy the lives of thousands of tiny air bubbles.

Part 5

## Baking: Rise Up And Cool Down *Without The Collapse*

*Chapter 20*

# Secrets to the Baking Phase

Many cupcakes bake at 350°F, 177°C for between 20-25 minutes. The baking time for mini cupcakes must be reduced by 5-7 minutes and increased by 5-10 minutes for large cupcakes. Recipes may differ in temperature and time requirements, so be sure to pay close attention to the baking time called for in the recipe in addition to ensuring your oven is at the proper temperature. If there is a time window, such as 25-30 minutes, check the cupcakes for doneness at or just before the minimum cooking time.

An oven thermometer helps you determine if your oven runs hotter, cooler or right on the mark for the temperature you set. Even brand new ovens can be off by 5°F, 2°C or more. The oven thermometer identifies how much off kilter your oven temperature can be, and can even identify hot spots in different areas of the oven. Set your oven so that the thermometer reads the correct temperature for your cupcake recipe.

Contrary to belief, your oven does not maintain an even heat throughout the time your cupcakes are baking. The oven produces heat in waves; the oven's built-in sensors monitor when the oven has reached the proper temperature and kicks the heating elements

The oven thermometer identifies how much off kilter your oven temperature can be, and can even identify hot spots in different areas of the oven.

You may need to adjust the oven racks prior to preheating the oven.

If they are too close, the cupcakes may brown unevenly and come out undercooked.

up higher when it senses heat reduction. The areas nearer the heating elements are prone to greater heat fluctuations.

You can prevent wide fluctuations in temperature that can cause your cupcakes to bake unevenly. First, open and close the oven door as quickly as is safe to do so when inserting the cupcakes for baking. Do not open the oven until the halfway point of minimum baking time has been reached. This is usually the 10 to 12 minute mark. When removing one batch to insert another, do not leave the oven gaping open like a gossip's mouth while you walk back and forth to switch cupcake tins. Have the next batch right next to the oven for a quick switch. Oven temperature can drop 25°F, 14°C even with a quick open and close cycle.

For best heat distribution and even baking, cupcakes should be placed in the center of the oven. You may need to adjust the oven racks prior to preheating the oven. As noted above, some ovens have hot spots, and most bakers do not do experiments to see if their oven has these hot spots, or where they might be located. Baking on the bottom rack could scorch the bottoms or scorch and cement your cupcakes to the liner bottom. Baking on the top rack near the broiler can scorch the top of the cakes.

For the best results, bake only one tray of cupcakes on one rack at a time. If you bake two trays of cupcakes together, put them on the same rack and not too close to each other. If they are too close, the cupcakes may brown unevenly and come out undercooked. If you do decide to bake two trays on different oven shelves, switch the pans of cupcakes halfway through baking time by moving the top pan to the bottom shelf and vice versa, and turning the cupcake pans around, too.

Avoid overbaking. Cupcakes are done when the moisture is just beginning to evaporate from the top and the cupcake tops spring back when touched. Cupcakes should be tested for doneness at the minimum baking time. You can do this by inserting a cake tester into the center of a cupcake to see if it is clean when you pull it out. You can also check it just as effectively by inserting a toothpick into the center. If the toothpick is clean or has a few tiny dry bits of cake, the cupcake is done. Another sign that the cupcakes are done is that cupcakes baked without paper liners have begun shrinking away from the sides of the cupcake wells.

When the cupcakes are golden brown, pulling away from the sides of the cupcake wells, and no longer wet in the center they are ready to come out of the oven and cool.

### Cupcake Cool Down

Cupcakes right out of the oven need to be removed from the pan and placed on a wire cooling rack within the first 3-5 minutes out of the oven. A wire rack is important because it allows air to circulate around all sides of the cupcake and prevents the cupcakes from overbaking and drying out if liners are not used. Removing the cupcakes

It takes cupcakes approximately 1-2 hours at normal room temperature (20°-22°C or 68°- 72°F) to completely cool down after baking.

from the pan within the first 3-5 minutes out of the oven also prevents the cupcake liners from separating from the cupcake. It takes cupcakes approximately 1-2 hours at normal room temperature (20°- 22°C or 68°- 72°F) to completely cool down after baking.

After the cupcakes are completely cooled down, they are spongy and golden brown. Now, they are cupcakes full of possibility, ready to be covered in brightly colored icing and sprinkles for a child's birthday party, graced with delicate frosting for an engagement party, or inserted into your mouth.

Your cupcakes are ready to frost...

171.

## Part 6

# Frostings, Glazes
# *And Icings*

*Chapter 21*

# All About Buttercreams, Whipped Cream Frostings and Pam Frostings

## Eggs in Frosting

Some recipes, like those mentioned in the upcoming Egg-White Frostings section, rely on whipped egg whites to give them structure and spreadability. Most of the buttercream frostings also depend heavily on eggs. The eggs in these recipes are either raw or partially cooked. Do not serve raw or partially cooked eggs to the very old, the very young, or to anyone who is pregnant or has a compromised immune system.

Especially avoid serving undercooked eggs if salmonella is a problem in your area. The safest way to prepare egg based frosting recipes is to use either dehydrated whole egg powder or powdered egg whites (available in some food stores and online at kingarthurflour.com, $7.95-$10.95, meringue powder $10.95). The FDA recommends that even dried egg products be cooked before being served to anyone with a significant risk (as described above).

To make the safest egg based frostings, you can purchase pasteurized liquid egg whites.

Pair lighter more delicate cupcakes with whipped cream or buttercream, and cream cheese frosting with buttery yellow, pumpkin cupcakes or your denser cupcake recipes.

To make the safest egg based frostings, you can purchase pasteurized liquid egg whites. If your local store does not have them in stock, they are available on Amazon.

## Pairing the Cupcake with the Frosting

Pair heavier frostings, like chocolate fudge, with cupcakes that are robust enough to support both the weight and the flavor. Pair lighter more delicate cupcakes with whipped cream or buttercream, and cream cheese frosting with buttery yellow pumpkin cupcakes or your denser cupcake recipes. One exception is Ganache, which goes well with anything other than chiffon type cupcakes.

### Buttercreams

Buttercreams are made of dreams. When you think of frosting, you probably think of buttercream. Rich, yet light, with just the right balance of sweetness and creaminess. Buttercream frosting is usually a mix of eggs and sugar that is partially cooked and whipped with butter and flavoring. Since butter is the name of the game in buttercream, using vegetable shortening is not a good idea. The only disadvantages to the traditionally made versions are the complicated preparation, the relatively short storage life, and the presence of raw or partially cooked eggs. (See the Eggs section.)

Even within the buttercream family there are significant variations. You can find a recipe for decorator buttercream in the Decorative Icings section. The other five are divided into two categories: those that use eggs – Italian, Swiss, and French; and those that do not – Simple and Golden.

**Italian Buttercream:** This cream incorporates a stream of hot sugar syrup as the egg whites are being whipped. (See Brown Sugar Buttercream recipe in the Appendix.)

**Swiss Buttercream:** Egg whites and sugar are whipped to a meringue while being cooked over a double boiler filled with hot water. This recipe produces a slightly drier frosting.

**French Buttercream:** Whole eggs are beaten over a double boiler. This is the richest of the three.

**Note:** These recipes contain partially cooked eggs. Please see the Eggs section for food safety information. Since the following buttercreams do not contain eggs, they store very well up to three weeks in the fridge. They can also be frozen.

**Simple Buttercream:** Popular with many home cooks for the extremely easy preparation, this is the sweetest of all buttercreams. Softened butter and sugar are beaten together with a small amount of liquid and a flavoring. (See Simple Buttercream recipe in the Appendix.)

**Golden Buttercream:** Simple Buttercream prepared with melted butter. Substitute 2 Tbsp. (17.36 g) of cornstarch for ½ cup (57.5 g) of powdered sugar.

The major drawback of whipped cream is that it neither keeps nor stores well. It also is very soft and cannot tolerate heat as well as a simple buttercream.

The delicately tangy taste and soft texture make sour cream frostings very popular for cupcakes based on popular coffee cakes and pastries.

## Whipped Cream Frostings

Whipped cream is a simple frosting. It is easy to make, readily available, and has a light and pleasant texture. The major drawback of whipped cream is that it neither keeps nor stores well. It also is very soft and cannot tolerate heat as well as a simple buttercream. It is often used in rich, sophisticated pastries and in Viennese-style tortes.

Some professional bakeries substitute non-dairy whipped topping such as Cool Whip. Although whipped topping is much more stable, there is a very noticeable taste difference. If you are planning on making authentic cupcake recipes, use real whipped cream.

## Cream Frostings

Sour cream and cream cheese frostings are also very common and relatively easy to make. The same method as simple buttercream is used, substituting cream cheese or sour cream for the butter.

Sour cream frostings are softer and more delicate than simple buttercream. They do not hold their shape very well and they tend to melt in a warm room. The delicately tangy taste and soft texture make sour cream frostings very popular for cupcakes based on popular coffee cakes and pastries.

Cream cheese based frostings are a little more robust. They tend to keep and store fairly well, and they can tolerate heat as well as a simple buttercream. There are two ways to make cream cheese frosting. One is using the simple buttercream method, as described above. Substitute cream cheese for the butter, mix with sugar and a small amount of liquid and add a flavoring. You'll need less liquid with cream cheese than with butter.

Another method is to whip softened cream cheese with vanilla extract and powdered sugar until it is light and airy, then fold in an equal amount of unsweetened whipped cream.  This method produces fluffy, rich frosting that is not too sweet and has a taste reminiscent of cheesecake, but that is more fragile and perishable than the cream produced with the Buttercream Method.

### Egg-White Frostings

Egg-white frostings are known as meringue frostings; they depend on whipped egg whites for body, structure and stability.  They are unique because they are virtually fat free.  This is why they are very light in texture, almost ethereal.

These frostings swirl and peak exceptionally well. Enriched with fruit, they are most memorably found in the Lady Baltimore Cupcake.  The Lady Baltimore cupcake, like the cake it is based on, is three layers of white cupcake frosted with Italian meringue icing. Chopped nuts and dried fruit such as raisins, figs, and pecans or almonds are mixed with the frosting.

Egg-white frostings are known as meringue frostings; they depend on whipped egg whites for body, structure, and stability.  They are unique because they are virtually fat free.

**Seven-Minute Frosting:** In a double boiler, egg whites and corn syrup are whipped over a hot water for seven minutes, after which they are removed from the heat. Vanilla is added, and the mixture is whipped for two minutes more.

**Boiled or Fluffy Frosting:** Like Italian buttercream, hot sugar syrup is whipped into egg whites to form a soft meringue. Add flavor and mix for two minutes.

**Note:** These recipes contain partially cooked eggs. Please see the Eggs section for food safety information.

*Chapter 22*

# Chocolate Frostings

Loosely speaking, chocolate frostings can be classified three ways: icing, Ganache, and buttercream. Icing and Ganache will be dealt with in later sections. In the chocolate buttercream family, there are several important divisions:

**Fudge:** Fudge frosting is very thick and rich. It is usually made with very dark chocolate, but milk chocolate or even white chocolate can be used. Fudge is the heaviest of all the frostings, and it is best suited to heavy cupcakes or brownies. It stores and freezes well.

**Chocolate Buttercream:** Lighter in texture, this is a simple buttercream that you add melted baker's chocolate to. It stores well and is very versatile and popular.

**Simple Chocolate Buttercream:** This is the lightest and sweetest of all buttercreams. Cocoa powder and additional sugar are creamed into a simple buttercream.

**White Chocolate Cream:** All of the butter in a simple buttercream is replaced by melted white chocolate.

Fudge is the heaviest of all the frostings, and it is best suited to heavy cupcakes or brownies. It stores and freezes well.

Made from chocolate shavings and hot milk or cream, and sometimes sugar and butter, Ganache stores and resists heat fairly well.

### Ganache

Somewhere between frosting and icing, Ganache is smooth, rich and chocolaty. Made from chocolate shavings and hot milk or cream, and sometimes sugar and butter, Ganache stores and resists heat fairly well. It is easy both to use and to make. Ganache can be used on all but the very lightest of cupcakes.

**Traditional Ganache:** Heavy cream is warmed and poured over shaved high-quality chocolate. It is beaten until smooth and allowed to cool slightly. White, dark, or milk chocolate can be used.

**Truffled Ganache:** Traditional Ganache is allowed to cool, then is whipped until light and fluffy, courtesy of the heavy cream becoming whipped cream. It can be used as a frosting or filling.

**Milk Chocolate Truffle:** Use milk chocolate shavings to make Truffled Ganache.

**White Truffle:** Use shaved white chocolate to make Truffled Ganache; add ½ tsp. (2.5 ml) of vanilla extract to the cream.

**Satin Ganache:** Hot milk is poured over shaved chocolate and stirred until chocolate melts. Butter and confectioner's sugar are added and it is beaten until smooth. This version is sweeter, shinier, and somewhat thicker.

**A Note About Whipping:** Take care when you beat or whip buttercreams or whipped cream based frostings.

Overwhipping cream can cause the frosting to separate and eventually form butter. Butter that is overbeaten becomes grainy. If you will be incorporating whipped cream into a frosting, as in the second cream cheese method, leave the cream a little bit on the soft side. It will be handled more as it is folded in. This should prevent any problems due to overwhipping.

Many butter or cream-based frostings are whipped to give them a fluffier texture, to increase the volume, or to reduce calories. In fact, the best secret to frosting with half the calories is to whip it up to twice the volume. Use the same amount to frost the cupcake and because the frosting volume is doubled, you have half the calories in the frosting! The best way to double the volume of frosting is to use a stand mixer with a balloon whisk attachment. Balloon whisks are specially designed to incorporate the maximum amount of air in the shortest possible time. If one is not available, a standard handheld mixer may be used. Whip only until the frosting is lighter in color and texture, but be very careful not to overbeat it.

Use the same amount to frost the cupcake and because the frosting volume is doubled, you have half the calories in the frosting!

*Chapter 23*

# Glazes and Icings

More or less interchangeable, glazes and icings are also called flat frostings. This is an excellent description because they are thin and often sheer. They are simply a mixture of confectioner's sugar and a liquid – usually water or milk, sometimes a fruit juice. A flavoring agent like vanilla extract or rum can also be added, as can cocoa powder. Glazes and icings are very simple to make; they handle the heat well, and they keep for long periods of time. Unless milk is used, they do not need to be refrigerated.

## Decorative Icings

Decorative icings, although not essential to the flavor of the cupcake, play a very important role in making it visually appealing. Many of the frostings already discussed are simply too soft to make decorations out of. Decorative icings can be molded into almost any form. They are made out of edible ingredients, although they are not meant to be eaten in quantity – or in the case of royal icing, at all. (We've all bitten into lovely frosting roses, only to find them dry and bitter. That was royal icing. If this is what the royalty eats…)

Glazes and icings are very simple to make; they handle the heat well, and they keep for long periods of time.

**Decorator's Buttercream:** It has a similar appearance to simple buttercream and is made the same way, but vegetable shortening replaces the butter. This gives the icing great stability and versatility, but many people find the waxy texture and taste of vegetable shortening unappealing.

**Fondant:** This sugary paste can be tinted, piped, rolled, molded, or draped over a cupcake. It is usually purchased either pre-made or in packaged form. The taste ranges from dull to sweet.

**Royal Icing:** This icing is made with egg whites and sugar that have been shaped into various decorations and dried. Many prefabricated decorations are readily available. This icing is not meant to be eaten.

## Specialty Frostings

Butter and sugar are staples of frosting. In some cases, they are the very essence. Although removing either one of them presents some challenges, it is possible to create frostings to suit various tastes and dietary needs.

**Non-Fat/Low-Fat:** If fat content is a concern, try making a sour cream frosting or a cream cheese frosting with low-fat or fat free products. Another very low-fat option is one of the Egg-White frostings. Remember to use dried egg whites.

**Dulce de Leche:** This delicious milk caramel can be used as a filling or frosting on its own, or it can be mixed into a simple buttercream. Whole milk and sugar are boiled together and allowed to reduce by approximately three-quarters. A pinch of baking soda is often added to prevent the sugar from crystallizing. It is rich, complex, easy to make, and time-consuming.

**Agave-Based Frostings:** The chief difficulty is controlling the texture of agave based frostings. As agave syrup replaces the sugar, the frosting is very soft. The flavor is unusual but pleasant, as is the frosting. (See the Agave Buttercream recipe.)

**Yogurt-Based Frostings:** Much like sour cream in taste, these frostings have a very soft texture. Honey is a natural addition to bring out the complexities of the yogurt. (See the recipe for Orange-Scented Yogurt Frosting.)

**Fruit:** Chopped fresh, candied, or dried fruit can be added to egg-white frostings to create endless variations of frostings and fillings. Fruit preserves or jams can be incorporated to simple buttercream. Try adding strawberry or cherry, or try combining peach and raspberry or fig and plum preserves.

**Dairy-Free:** Omitting the milk and butter from a simple buttercream can make a simple, lactose-free frosting. Substitute it with coconut milk and coconut oil – a white, solid vegetable fat that is available at many grocery stores. The egg-white frostings are also non-dairy. You can use agar for a thickener if the coconut oil is soft or liquid.

As agave syrup replaces the sugar, the frosting is very soft. The flavor is unusual but pleasant, as is the frosting.

Fruit preserves or jams can be incorporated to simple buttercream.

# Frosting and Icing Chart

The following table summarizes the properties of the frostings.

| FROSTING | FAST | EASY | SWEET | ADVANTAGES | DISADVANTAGES |
|---|---|---|---|---|---|
| Italian Buttercream | No | No | Moderately | Superior Flavor and Texture | Eggs Not Fully Cooked; Must be Refrigerated |
| Swiss Buttercream | No | No | Moderately | Superior Flavor and Texture | Eggs Not Fully Cooked; Must be Refrigerated |
| French Buttercream | No | No | Moderately | Superior Flavor and Texture | Eggs Not Fully Cooked; Must be Refrigerated |
| Simple Buttercream | Yes | Yes | Very | Sweet and Buttery | May Be Overly Sweet |
| Golden Buttercream | Yes | Yes | Yes | Rich Flavor | Slightly Soft Texture |
| Whipped Cream | Yes | Yes | Moderately | Light, Rich Flavor | Hard to Store |
| Sour Cream | Yes | Yes | Yes | Distinctive Flavor | Soft Texture |
| Cream Cheese | Yes | Yes | Yes^ | Distinctive Flavor | Slightly Stiff Texture |
| 7-Minute Frosting | No | Moderately | Yes | Light and Fluffy, Low-fat, Dairy-Free | May Be Overly Sweet; Eggs Not Fully Cooked; Must be Refrigerated |
| Boiled/Fluffy Frosting | No | Moderately | Yes | Light and Fluffy, Low-fat, Dairy-Free | May Be Overly Sweet; Eggs Not Fully Cooked; Must be Refrigerated |
| Chocolate Buttercream | Yes | Yes | Moderately | Light, Buttery, | None |
| Fudge Frosting | Moderately | Moderately | Yes | Chocolaty | Dense, Heavy Texture |
| Simple Chocolate Buttercream | Yes | Yes | Yes | Rich and Intense | May Be Overly Sweet |
| White Chocolate Buttercream | Yes | Yes | Yes | Light, Sweet and Flexible | May Be Overly Sweet |

The following table summarizes the properties of the frostings.

| FROSTING | FAST | EASY | SWEET | ADVANTAGES | DISADVANTAGES |
|---|---|---|---|---|---|
| Traditional Ganache | Moderately | Yes | Moderately | Light, Sweet and Flexible | Not Thick or Fluffy |
| Truffled Ganache | Moderately | Moderately | Moderately | Rich and Smooth | Must be Refrigerated |
| Satin Ganache | Moderately | Moderately | Yes | Thick, Rich and Fluffy | Not Thick or Fluffy |
| Glazes/Icings | Yes | Yes | Very | Rich, Shiny and Smooth | Flat-tasting |
| Decorator's Buttercream | Yes | Yes | NA | Sweet | Waxy |
| Fondant | Yes | Yes* | Moderately^ | NA | Waxy |
| Royal Icing | No# | Yes* | NA | Moldable | NA |
| Dulce de Leche | No | Yes | Yes | NA | Very Soft Texture |
| Agave Frosting | Moderately | No | Yes^ | Complex, Smooth, Rich | Very Soft Texture; Very Sweet^ |
| Yogurt Frosting | No | Moderately | Moderately | Sugar-Free | Very Soft Texture; Must Be Refrigerated |
| | | | | Interesting, Unique Flavor | |

| | |
|---|---|
| * | Although easy to make, these may not be easy to work with. |
| ^ | Taste varies based on method used. |
| # | Royal Frosting must be dried overnight. |
| NA | These frostings are not meant to be eaten. |

# Part 7

## Advanced
## *Cupcaking*

*Chapter 24*

# Create Your Own Cupcake Recipes from Scratch

Cupcake recipes cannot be created by mixing a little of this and a little of that like seasoning a main dish. Baking is chemistry, a delicate science of sweetness. There are definite rules to follow. Following the rules of cupcake science will free you to create an infinite number of sensational and unforgettable cupcake recipes.

There are ingredient proportions that, if followed, give you the right result every time. There are the cupcake equations. As covered in the What Ingredients Do section, the main components of cupcake recipes are the structure, tenderizers, moisturizers and leaveners. If you have too much of one component and not enough of another within the baking chemistry ratios you will have a cupcake wreck on your hands.

Whether to substitute ingredients like non-gluten flour, reduce the fat or swap sugar components, you will need to know these ratios.

The main ingredients that give a cupcake structure are the flour and the eggs. Not enough structure ingredients and you have soft, liquidy cupcakes or cupcakes that fall

Following the rules of cupcake science will free you to create an infinite number of sensational and unforgettable cupcake recipes.

If you have too much of one component and not enough of another within the baking chemistry ratios you will have a cupcake wreck on your hands.

apart. Too much of the structure building ingredients and you will have tough, dry cupcakes.

Use the following formulas together to create the right mixture for your own traditional cupcake recipes. These do not cover egg foam or sponge cake recipes that do not contain fat. These formulas are guidelines and not exact parameters. These guidelines can vary slightly within a 20% range and be fine. However, calculate twice and mix once. If you do find you have a problem, move back closer to the ratio guidelines.

**The Flour/Sugar Ratio** – The recipe should have an approximate 1 to 1 ratio of flour to sugar in weight – or a slightly higher sugar to flour ratio. If you are not baking by weight, reference the Weight & Measurement Chart for quick conversions. A cup of sugar weighs 7.1 ounces or 201 grams, and a cup of cake flour weighs 3.67 ounces or 104 grams.

**The Eggs/Butter Ratio** – Additionally, the shelled eggs need to weigh approximately the same or a bit more than the weight of the fat in the recipe. A large egg weighs approximately 1¾ ounces or 50 grams. Add 2 ounces of butter or shortening per egg. So, for 4 ounces of butter or shortening, you can use 2 eggs. A yolk from a large egg weighs 2/3 of an ounce or 19 grams. To create a smoother, creamier mouth feel and a moister cupcake you can add a yolk. Using all egg whites will create a drier texture.

**The Eggs and Liquid to Sugar Ratio –** The liquid and the eggs need to weigh as much or slightly more than the weight of the sugar you use in the recipe.

**Chemical Leavening –** Add 1 tsp. (4 g) of baking powder per cup of cake flour, 3.67 ounces (104 grams). If the recipe has a lot of acidic ingredients such as buttermilk, sour cream, citrus juice (lemon, lime, orange), you should add ¼ tsp. of baking soda (1 g).

**Flavor Enhancing –** Salt really kicks up the sweetness in your cupcake recipe. Add just ½ tsp. (3 g) of salt for each cup of flour (120 grams) to help create your own unforgettable cupcake recipes.

*Chapter 25*

# How to Create Filled and Stuffed Cupcakes Like a Pro

What can be better than a cupcake, piled high with frosting and imaginatively decorated? What can be better than a cupcake that has been frosted, decorated, and filled or stuffed with a luscious center?

Crème-filled cupcakes have become commonplace in bakeries and in mass-production. Home cookbooks have surprisingly little to say on the subject. Even respected volumes like *The New Basics Cookbook, Better Homes and Gardens New Cookbook,* and Le Cordon Bleu's *Complete Cooking Techniques* don't mention how to create filled cupcakes. That leaves the question that everyone, young or old, asks: How does the filling get *inside* the cupcake, anyway?

It is not as complicated as it first appears. Following are five of the best methods for creating filled or stuffed cupcakes presented in a step-by-step format. Soon you will be in on all the secrets of how to whip up your own delectable filled and stuffed cupcakes!

How does the filling get *inside* the cupcake, anyway?

A Ziploc sandwich bag with the tip cut off of one corner can also be used to frost your cupcakes if you do not own pastry bags or decorating tools.

## The Difference between Filling and Stuffing

What's the difference between filling and stuffing? Easy. Filling happens after baking and stuffing before; stuffings are also usually created from dry ingredients rather than from creams.

## Professional Tips to Filling Cupcakes

### Preparation

Before you start filling the cupcakes, check the following things:

- Are your cupcakes completely cool?
- Is your chosen filling at a spreadable consistency?
- If you are using a pastry bag or other decorating tool, make sure it is clean and properly assembled. A Ziploc sandwich bag with the tip cut off of one corner can also be used to frost your cupcakes if you do not own pastry bags or decorating tools.

### The Basics about Fillings

Fillings fall into four categories:

1. **Creamy fillings**, such as whipped cream, frosting, ice cream and pudding
2. **Fruit fillings**, like jam, pie filling, or fresh fruit
3. **Combined fillings**, such as grated chocolate added to a creamy base filling

4. **Heavy fillings** like cream cheese or peanut
   butter

Don't be afraid to try a variety of fillings and make up your own! Keep in mind the following points:

### Creamy fillings

Do not attempt to bake whipped cream, frosting, pudding, or ice cream into the cupcakes. Soft cream-type fillings melt at high temperatures. If you make a combined filling that uses one of these as a base, the same rule applies.

### Fruit fillings

If you choose to fill baked cupcakes with jam or fruit preserves, drain as much excess liquid as possible. Jam needs to be warmed before piping; to do this, spoon the jam into the pastry bag and work it with your hands for a few moments. It will soon become soft enough to use. Work quickly, though, because it will shortly rc-gcl.

Jams and fruit fillings withstand heat somewhat better than creamy fillings, but it is not advisable to bake them; they may become overly runny, chewy, unpleasantly crispy, or gummy. The excess liquid may also cause the cupcake to be soggy. An exception, of course, is the type of pie filling that is designed to be baked. Drain off all excess liquids first and be aware that the fruit might shrink or shrivel during cooking.

Jams and fruit fillings withstand heat somewhat better than do creamy fillings, but it is not advisable to bake them; they may become overly runny, chewy, unpleasantly crispy, or gummy.

### Heavy fillings

Heavy fillings like nut butters or cream cheese may need to be lightened, especially if you are using the insertion method. For fillings that will remain unbaked, try adding whipped topping, whipped cream, or vanilla frosting. Or thin the base filling with milk and add powdered sugar until it is creamy and smooth. This also works well for baked fillings, as does the addition of whipped egg whites and sugar.

*Chapter 26*

# Professional Cupcake Filling and Stuffing Methods

There are five primary methods of filling cupcakes:
1. The insertion method
2. The removal method
3. The layering method
4. The partially-baked method
5. The self-filling method

### Insertion Method

Filling Amount: Moderate
Filling Type: Creamy, Fruit, Combined
Difficulty Level: Easy
Equipment: Pastry bag fitted with a wide star-type decorating tip

1. Using a clean finger or the tip of the pastry bag, poke a hole in the top of the cupcake.
2. Insert the tip to the bottom of the hole and squeeze gently while slowly lifting until filling is level with the top of the cupcake.

3. If you wish, finish frosting the cupcake by moving the pastry bag in a circular motion while continuing to squeeze gently.

### Removal Method

Filling Amount:  Moderate to Full
Filling Type:  Creamy, Fruit, Combined
Difficulty:  Moderate
Equipment:  Pastry bag, small-bladed knife

1. With the knife (a paring knife or a similar knife with a thin, short blade would be best; a butter knife can be used), remove a section of the top of the cupcake.  The bigger the section removed, the more filling will go inside the cupcake.
2. Fill the cavity with the desired filling, using a pastry bag (or a sandwich bag with the corner clipped off). Do not fill up to the level of the top of the cupcake.
3. Cut a slice off the top of the removed section; place on top of the filling and press down slightly, until it is level with the top of the cupcake.
4. Frost, ice or decorate as usual.

Note:  If you have one, use an apple corer to hollow out an area for the filling.  Use the same directions as above.

The two methods discussed above work best with light, creamy fillings or jam.  Combined fillings may be used in either method, but a wide-tipped pastry bag is needed.  Chunky combined fillings (nut creams, nut pastes, cannoli-type filling, etc.) are most suited to the removal method.  To fill, use a spoon, a Ziploc sandwich bag with a larger cut, or a pastry bag with no tip attached.  Cupcakes with very chunky fillings, like whipped cream and whole cherries, benefit most from the layering method.

### Layering Method

Filling Amount:  Variable
Filling Type:  Combined, Heavy
Difficulty:  Moderately Hard
Equipment:  Butter knife, Paring knife

Using the paring knife, cut the cupcake in thirds, horizontally.

1. Base layer first:  Frost the top surface with the butter knife.  If using fruit or candy, press a piece or two into the filling you just spread.
2. Second layer:  Frost the bottom surface, place it on top of the base layer and press slightly.
3. Frost the top of the second layer.  Press another piece of fruit or candy into the filling.
4. Final layer: Lightly frost the underside of the final layer and press it down gently onto the second layer.

Cupcakes with very chunky fillings, like whipped cream and whole cherries, benefit most from the layering method.

Allowing the cupcake to start baking before the filling is added gives the dough the necessary structure to support the filling.

5. Frost the top of the cupcake and decorate it with more candy or a piece of fruit.

The layering method has the advantage of incorporating a wide range of ingredients into the cupcake – here, creativity could be boundless – but depending on the amount of ingredients and fillings used, the cupcake can become unstable. It may tilt or lean unattractively, and it definitely is harder to eat. In short, it is more of a particularly diminutive layered cupcake cake, and agile eaters may enjoy the unusual look.

The final two filling methods blur the line between filling and stuffing. (As mentioned above, filling happens after baking and stuffing before; stuffings are also usually created from dry ingredients rather than from creams.) In the fourth method, the cupcake is partially baked before the filling is added. Because the filling is heavier and denser than the unbaked cake batter, any filling added would fall to the bottom of the cupcake.

**TIP:** Allowing the cupcake to start baking before the filling is added gives the dough the necessary structure to support the filling.

The fifth method is self-filling: A separate filling is dropped into the cupcake immediately before baking. Properly so, this is considered stuffing, not filling, but the finished product is actually a cross between pudding and cheesecake in texture.

## Partially-Baked Method

Filling Amount:  Moderate
Filling Type:  Heavy Fillings, Candy, Fruit
Difficulty Level:  Moderately Easy
Equipment:  Small-sized melon baller or spoon

1.  Fill the lined (or oiled) cupcake wells halfway.
2.  Bake between 10-15 minutes, until cupcakes are well-risen but wobbly.
3.  Using a scoop or a spoon, drop 1 scant Tbsp. (15 ml) of filling into each cupcake.
4.  Finish baking.
5.  Allow to fully cool.
6.  Frost as usual.

## Self-Filling Method

Filling Amount:  Moderate
Filling Type:  Heavy
Difficulty Level:  Easy
Equipment:  Large spoon or medium-sized melon baller.

1.  Prepare cupcakes according to recipe.
2.  Fill lined (or oiled) cupcake wells halfway.
3.  Add melon ball size of filling to each cupcake.
4.  Bake as directed.
5.  Let cool completely.
6.  Frost as usual.

The Partially Baked and Self-Filling methods should only be used for firm fillings, such as those based on peanut butter or cream cheese.

### Bonus Recipe for High End Filling

8 oz softened mascarpone
Pasteurized egg mixture = 1 egg
1/3 cup (64 g/2.26 oz) superfine sugar
6 oz (170.1 g) grated semi-sweet chocolate (a 6 oz chocolate bar)
1 tsp. pure vanilla extract

Mix the mascarpone and pasteurized egg together. Then add in the superfine sugar and vanilla extract. Finally, mix in the grated chocolate until well mixed.

Drop a glob approximately the size of a rounded soup spoon into unbaked cupcakes; bake as directed.

*Fills approximately 24 cupcakes*

**Note:** This filling will be very soft when uncooked. To make it easier to scoop out, allow to chill before using.

### Ice Cream Filled Cupcakes

Filling cupcakes with ice cream is fun, easy, and always a crowd-pleaser. Use the first or second method for filling the cakes.

Allow the ice cream to soften until it is like frosting. Stir it occasionally while it does so to make sure it is smooth and lump-free. Keep a close eye on it so it doesn't get too close to the runny stage. Working quickly, pipe the ice cream into the cupcakes. If desired, frost with more ice cream.

Refreeze until the ice cream begins to harden, at least 20 minutes. (These steps may be done several days ahead.)

Thaw for 5 minutes before serving.

If you haven't already frosted the cupcakes with ice cream, top them with whipped cream, hot fudge and a cherry just before serving.

### Stuffed Cupcakes

The partially baked and self-filling methods under filling methods above may also be used for stuffing a cupcake. Popular stuffings include streusel, fruit, small candies, or nuts and nut butters. Stuffings like candy (but not chocolate), nuts, and fruit are usually tossed with a small amount of flour or boxed cake mix before they are added to raw batter so that they remain suspended in the cake and do not fall to the bottom. When the cupcake is partially baked, though, flouring the stuffings is not necessary.

Stuffings like candy (but not chocolate), nuts, and fruit are usually tossed with a small amount of flour or boxed cake mix before they are added to raw batter so that they remain suspended in the cake and do not fall to the bottom.

**Ten Ideas for Stuffing Cupcakes**

1. Hershey's Hugs or Kisses
2. Reese's (mini-sized)
3. Junior Mints
4. Chocolate Truffles
5. Trail Mix
6. Fresh Pitted Cherries
7. Caramels
8. Chocolate-Covered Cherries
9. Fresh Hulled Strawberries and 10 Chocolate Brownie Chunks

Filled and stuffed cupcakes, impressive and delectable, remain well within your reach – and not just in arm's reach at the grocery store. With a little patience and a trial batch or two, you can reliably create fun, surprising little cupcakes for which taste buds everywhere will stand up and cheer.

If a cupcake does not have frosting, is it still a cupcake? The general opinion is yes, it is a cupcake, but whether it is worth eating is a matter of conscience. Frosting is, quite literally, the icing on the cupcake.

At its most basic recipe, frosting is a combination of fat and/or eggs, sugar, and a flavoring agent. Scientifically-minded bakers, ignoring the obvious, will detail its ability to seal in moisture or will explain that it has a pleasant mouth-feel and it enhances the flavor of the cupcake. All of this is true, but it misses the main point: Frosting simply tastes good. Since frosting is such an umbrella word, are there really all that many different types of frosting? Does it matter which frosting is used with which cupcake?

The answers are yes and yes. There are nine major categories of frosting and icing. The ninth category, specialty frostings, will explain how to create frostings that are low in fat, dairy-free, or based on unorthodox ingredients like yogurt or agave. There is also a summary chart that compares the characteristics and various sweetness levels of the different frosting types.

Part 8

# How To Store, Transport And *Ship Cupcakes*

*Chapter 27*

# Storing and Freezing Cupcakes

Storing, transporting and shipping cupcakes are some of the most important topics to think about when you need to move your cupcakes from one place to another. Cupcakes normally don't linger anywhere long, uneaten. And, unless you freeze them, cupcakes need to be eaten within 3 days. So, if they have to go traveling, you want to make sure that after all your hard work they arrive just as beautiful as they were when you packed them.

Considering their popularity as gifts, or at bake sales, parties, and showers, cupcakes are on the move more than ever.  Is it possible to ship a cupcake (via mail, as opposed to using a pack-and-ship service) that will, in fact, still *be* a cupcake when it arrives at its destination? The secrets for getting cupcakes shipped successfully overnight, priority mail or down the block are the only thing between "oooos" and "aaahhhhs" and a "what the heck?" at their destination. Should they be refrigerated or frozen before hand?  Discover how to store cupcakes, pack them for local trips, display them, and ship them. A summary of two unique shipping ideas is next.

Considering their popularity as gifts, or at bake sales, parties, and showers, cupcakes are on the move more than ever.

Tightly covered tops will become sticky.

To prevent the wrap from sticking to frosted cupcakes, freeze them for an hour, stick a toothpick in the top, then wrap them.

## Storing Cupcakes

The tips below are excellent general tips about cupcake storage.

Cupcakes must be completely cooled before frosting, covering, or storing. Cover unfrosted cupcakes loosely so that the tops stay dry. Tightly covered tops will become sticky. Frosted cupcakes may be refrigerated for three days; unfrosted will stay fresh up to five days in the fridge.

Refrigerate cupcakes that are frosted with whipped cream or have creamy fillings. Loosely cover frosted cupcakes with wax paper and store them in a cake safe, an inverted box, or clean and reusable or disposable plastic cake container. If at all possible, frost cupcakes the day they will be eaten. To prevent the wrap from sticking to frosted cupcakes, freeze them for an hour, stick a toothpick in the top, then wrap them.

## Freezing Cupcakes

Cupcakes freeze well. In fact, frozen cupcakes will stay fresher than those that have been stored in the refrigerator. Those tend to dry out after five days. The simplest way to freeze cupcakes is to leave them unfrosted and wrap them well in cling wrap. Freeze the frosting separately in a plastic bag. Allow both to fully thaw. Cut away a corner of the frosting bag and pipe the frosting onto the cupcakes, then dispose of the bag.

Of course, frosted cupcakes can still be frozen. Freeze them unwrapped first; once the frosting is hard, wrap them tightly. If you plan to freeze the cupcakes, avoid decorating with hard candies (such as Red Hots), sprinkles, decorating gel, colored sugar or anything that will melt or run when thawed. Coconut or chocolate chips are fine. They will keep in the freezer for at least two months.

Finally, be sure to let your recipient know to defrost them slowly. Overnight in the fridge is probably the best choice. Be sure they don't use an oven or a microwave to thaw the cupcakes. The wrapping should be removed immediately from the cupcakes so they stay dry.

## Individually Wrapping Cupcakes

The primary problems in wrapping cupcakes are keeping the cake fresh and keeping the frosting intact. Wrapping them tightly will keep the cake from drying out, but it will decimate the frosting. If you are shipping your cupcakes or selling them individually, like at a bake sale, wrap them individually. To protect the frosting, try covering it with coconut, rolling it in sprinkles, or using a royal frosting decoration, such as a rose. Otherwise, use one of the wrapping methods below.

If you plan to freeze the cupcakes, avoid decorating with hard candies (such as Red Hots), sprinkles, decorating gel, colored sugar, or anything that will melt or run when thawed.

To protect the frosting, try covering it with coconut, rolling it in sprinkles, or using a royal frosting decoration, such as a rose.

## Wrapping an Unfrosted Cupcake

Place the cupcake, top down, on a square of cling wrap. Placing a piece of waxed paper between the top of the cupcake and the cling wrap will protect the flavor. Crumpling it will keep the cupcake from getting sticky.

Pull in each of the four sides of the cling wrap and smooth them down to seal out any air. Make sure there are no exposed spaces.

If the edges tend to come apart, secure them with a piece of tape along the bottom of the cupcake.

## Wrapping a Frosted Cupcake

Place 1-2 toothpicks at the peak of the frosting. Stick 2-4 more toothpicks horizontally along the base of the frosting, roughly where the four corners would be if the cupcake bottom was square.

Drape a large square of plastic wrap over the toothpicks and down to the bottom of the cupcake. Seal all four corners using a piece of tape if necessary.

Another option is to freeze the entire cupcake uncovered until the frosting is hard, then wrap the whole thing. Finally, instead of using cling wrap, consider using a lidded plastic cup. Place the cupcake on the lid and place the cup over the cupcake. (Please see the final section for more information on this technique.)

Now that the cupcakes are firmly wrapped, it's time to go places. Other than carrying them in two at a time or really messing up your new briefcase, what options are available for cases?

## Cupcake Carrying Cases

Commercially produced carrying cases are sturdy, easy to clean, and readily available both online and in stores. If you frequently bake and share your cupcakes, these can be good choices for both storing and transporting your little desserts. If, however, you plan on mailing them or giving them as gifts, buying a new carrying case each time can get a little pricey.

*Chapter 28*

# Homemade and Reusable Cupcake Shipping Containers

Fashioning a homemade cupcake carrying case can be as simple as putting the cupcakes back in their baking tin, covering them with an upside-down rectangular baking/cake pan, and securing the pan with clips or tape. Shipping such a heavy weight would be expensive, as would purchasing new bakeware every time you ship cupcakes to some lucky soul.

The following options are inexpensive, portable, and replaceable:

- Use cardboard cases that have built-in dividers, such as soda cases; wrap the cupcakes or cover the top of the case with cling wrap.
- Secure the cupcakes to the bottom of a cardboard box with double-sided tape. Of course, this double stick tape method assumes you bake the cupcakes with cupcake liners.
- Pack them into a disposable aluminum roasting pan and cover it with another pan or cling wrap, taking care not to let the frosting touch the top, sides, or another cupcake.

Fashioning a homemade cupcake carrying case can be as simple as putting the cupcakes back in their baking tin, covering them with an upside-down rectangular baking/cake pan, and securing the pan with clips or tape.

When packing cupcakes for a car journey, it is especially important to make sure they will not slide around, turn over, or smash into each other or the side of the container.

- Reuse a disposable plastic cake container, packing the cupcakes in the top and using the flat bottom as a lid.

## Packaging Cupcakes for a Car Ride

When packing cupcakes for a car journey, it is especially important to make sure they will not slide around, turn over, or smash into each other or the side of the container. If possible, carry the cupcakes unfrosted and take a few minutes to frost them when you arrive. If the cupcakes are for a party, consider a cupcake buffet; offer several choices of frostings and toppings and let everyone create their own!

## Packing Cupcakes for Shipping

If a car journey is perilous, sending your cupcakes winging into the vast unknown, or sending them by mail is even more dangerous. Unless you are willing to pay for a pack-and-ship service to securely send them for you, be prepared to be additionally careful.

First, wrap each cupcake in cling wrap. It is imperative that the cupcakes are not able to move around freely. Either fasten the bottoms with double-sided tape and fill the spaces with packing peanuts or use some kind of divider, as discussed in the section Cupcake Carrying Cases.

Use a sturdy cardboard box. If possible, put the cupcakes in one box and place that box in one slightly larger. Mark the box FRAGILE and THIS SIDE UP. Delivery times vary according to postal class.  While overnight or next-day delivery is the fastest, it is also the most expensive. Treating the box as a parcel will practically guarantee rough treatment and slow shipping.  For many, the best option is the flat-rate boxes offered by the USPS Priority Mail service.  Find the box that best suits the number of cupcakes you need to ship.

Don't forget the ever inventiveness of your fellow cupcake bakers; they're a smart, creative community. New ideas come up all the time.

## Traveling Cupcakes

Packing cupcakes for a trip around town is easy compared to shipping them without investing a small fortune in packing materials like the cupcake bakeries use.

The brilliant idea of packing the cupcake in an individual plastic cup container with a lid was invented by Clara, the author of iheartcuppycakes.com. After drinking a caramel macchiato from Starbucks, Clara came up with this brilliant do-it-yourself shipping solution.  The object of this experiment was to make packaging stable enough to withstand the ultimate shipping challenge—a trip to Afghanistan.

Here is how to do it.
1.  Bake your cupcakes in plain white party nut cups, which are sturdier than the paper cupcake liners.
2.  Let cool all the way.

Bake your cupcakes in plain white party nut cups, which are sturdier than the paper cupcake liners.

3. Frost the cupcakes leaving the sides of the cupcake unfrosted. If you frost the sides of the cupcakes, that part will get smashed during packing.

4. Freeze the cupcakes overnight to set the frosting. You need to use a frosting that can be easily frozen. (See the frosting chart.)

5. Once frozen, individually wrap each frosted cupcake securing the plastic wrap edges at the base of the cupcakes, leaving a bit of room on top of the frosting to allow for the expansion that defrosting brings.

6. Next, take clear plastic tall cups and turn them upside down over the plastic wrapped cupcakes and secure the bottom of each cupcake to the edge of the cups with stickers.

7. Put the cupcakes in a box separated by a cardboard divider to keep them separated. If the divider does not fit exactly, either trim the divider to fit or pad the edge with newspaper or tissue paper. Choose a box that is slightly higher than the cups. The plastic wrap around the cupcake, the sticker securing the cupcake to the edge of the plastic cup, and the shape of the cup (narrowing) will keep the cupcakes from moving around during shipping. The divider and closely matching height of the box to the cups will keep your cupcakes from moving around.

8. Wrap the box as required per shipping requirements for the shipper you choose, and ship!

9. Overnight shipping is recommended.
10. Clara provides step-by-step pictures for the entire process. http://iheartcuppycakes.com/2008/03/13/how-to-ship-a-cupcake-solution/ Shipping cupcakes is not inexpensive.

Storing, packing and shipping cupcakes may not be as much fun as eating them. However, once the specific challenges that confront each step are understood, they can be successfully overcome.

You can store cupcakes in the freezer for long periods of time. The cupcakes will stay fresh up to three months if you wrap them in plastic wrap and freeze them in an airtight container. Unless you are freezing the cupcakes to ship as described previously, it is best to freeze the frosting separately and decorate the cakes later. As long as you don't use anything that will discolor the frosting while it thaws, then you can freeze them fully-frosted.

Cupcakes will last for five days on the countertop if properly covered or wrapped, as long as the room temperature is 68°-72°F or 20°-22°C. Remember to refrigerate cupcakes that have cream-based fillings or frosting; they will stay fresh in the fridge for five days.

Freezing a frosted cupcake uncovered for an hour will make it easier to wrap. Consider topping the frosting with coconut flakes or grated chocolate, or use toothpicks or decorations to protect the frosting. Wrap all cupcakes securely if you are planning on shipping them.

The cupcakes will stay fresh up to three months if you wrap them in plastic wrap and freeze them in an airtight container.

Cupcakes will last for five days on the countertop if properly covered or wrapped, as long as the room temperature is 68°-72°F or 20°-22°C.

Many cupcake carriers are available to help you transport your cupcakes around town. You can also make your own, but make sure all the cupcakes are firmly in place before traveling. Unless you are pressed for time, an easy option is to transport the cupcakes unfrosted and decorate them on site.

Shipping cupcakes can be daunting, given the rough handling and differing timelines involved. With some ingenuity, a few plastic cups, and some double-sided tape, though, constructing a relatively light, low-cost cupcake mailer is a very good solution.

## Displaying Cupcakes

If the cupcakes are for a bake sale, you set them out for display. It is never a good idea to leave them uncovered or unwrapped. If they will be for sale individually, wrap them individually. If this is not possible, or if they will be sold as a group, pack them in a pan and cover the pan with clear cling wrap (see the third suggestion under Cupcake Carrying Cases).

Part 9

# MASTERING THE ART OF
## *Unforgettable Cupcakes*

*Chapter 29*

# Frequently Asked Questions & Troubleshooting

**How can I get the paper to stop sticking to the cupcake? It happens every time!**

It is very important to remove the cupcakes from the pan at the 3-5 minute mark after baking.  Otherwise, steam forms between the cake and the liner, resulting in stickiness and an overly soft texture.

**Is it better to use Silicone, foil, or paper wrappers, or no wrappers at all?**

Using liners is usually preferable to using unlined cupcake wells.  It is much easier to remove the cupcake – and clean the baking tin – when liners have been used. They also keep the cupcake moist and fresh longer.  (For more information about foil and paper liners, see the following question.)

Silicone liners are also non-stick, and they have the eco-friendly advantage of being reusable.  If you want to use Silicone liners without a cupcake tin, make sure to buy the thickest ones.

Using liners is usually preferable to using unlined cupcake wells. It is much easier to remove the cupcake – and clean the baking tin – when liners have been used.  They also keep the cupcake moist and fresh longer.

Most cupcake recipes are based on large eggs.

**When baking cupcakes, what difference does it make if you use paper or foil baking cups? Does it affect the cooking time?**

There is no change to the baking time. The difference between foil and paper liners is largely cosmetic. Many cooks like the wide variety of patterns and designs available with paper liners. Some also feel that foil liners photograph better, since they reflect a lot of light. Fans of foil liners feel that the shiny silver makes a cupcake look classier and hides grease marks.

**Is it better to use cupcake paper cups or just pour the batter directly into the pan after greasing them?**

Paper cupcake liners do two things: They make it easier to get the cupcake out of the well in one piece and they protect the cake itself, keeping it clean and moist. Unless you intend to serve the cupcakes later that same day, use a liner.

**If a recipe calls for eggs, what size are they talking about if they don't specify?**

Most cupcake recipes are based on large eggs. (Please see the egg size table on page 29 for information on substituting different sizes.)

**If you only have jumbo eggs and a recipe for cupcakes calls for 2 eggs, how many jumbo eggs should you use?**

In a word, two. The following chart shows the various egg sizes and equivalents, based on large eggs.

## Different Egg Size Equivalents Chart

| # of Eggs in Recipe | Small | Medium | Extra-Large | Jumbo |
|---|---|---|---|---|
| 1 (Large) Egg | 1 | 1 | 1 | 1 |
| 2 | 3 | 2 | 2 | 2 |
| 3 | 4 | 3 | 3 | 2 |
| 4 | 5 | 5 | 4 | 3 |
| 5 | 7 | 6 | 4 | 4 |

**How do you ensure that cupcakes come out really moist? My cupcakes are always on the dry side even when I follow the recipe.**

Several things may be at fault here.  There may be too much leavening, too much oil/shortening or egg, or the recipe may not be mixed properly.  It is also a good idea to use cake flour instead of all-purpose flour, and be sure to sift it.  (If the recipe specifically calls for all-purpose flour, to substitute cake flour add 1½ Tbsp. (9.75 g) in addition to each cup (104 g/3.67 oz) of cake flour.) Or, for every 120 g (4.23 oz) of all-purpose flour use 113.75 g (4.01 oz) of cake flour. Finally, always bake the cupcakes in the middle of the oven. Rotate the cupcake pans halfway through baking if necessary. This may increase the baking time just a smidge, since the oven temperature drops at least 25°F, 14°C any time you open the oven door.

**What other ingredients or techniques can be used to make cupcakes moist and soft?**

First, follow the recipe exactly, including the order that the ingredients are added, mixed, and blended.

Also, be sure to cream the butter and sugar thoroughly together. This means going beyond the creaming you do when you make cookie dough. The batter for cupcakes should be creamed until the volume increases and the sugar granules dissolve. This takes 8 to 10 minutes (yes, I'm serious), by adding a heaping spoonful of sugar to room temperature butter. Recipes that use the creaming technique don't usually call for the full 8-10 minutes because recipe inventors know that you might never try an awesome new recipe if you see it needs the butter and sugar creamed for so long.

Here's a little secret: If you spend the time to cream, you will create a tender, delicate texture. Also, if you use superfine sugar, the time to blend will be reduced. The secret to blending the two together without spending 8-10 minutes? Beat room temperature butter on medium with superfine sugar until ridges begin to form in the mixture.

At that point, it is completely blended. You don't want to over mix, because the butter will begin to break down and lose the ability to hold air bubbles.

You can also substitute buttermilk for milk or water to make the cakes especially moist; the acid in the buttermilk increases the moisture held by the cupcakes as they bake. You can also substitute banana puree, sour cream or mayonnaise for half of the butter. These ingredients also retain moisture very well. If using the banana puree, reduce sugar by 2 Tbsp. (25.125 g) and increase flour by 1 Tbsp. (7.5 g).

**Why do they come out different, sometimes too soft, and they stick to the pan even though you always use the same recipe?**

Are they always being made in the same spot, in the same oven, with the exact same ingredients? Any one of these things may vary, quite unknowingly, to the cook. Another factor is the weather. Sometimes high humidity spoils the texture of cakes, causing them to either toughen or fall. Using a different cupcake pan can also affect the outcome, if the type of pan requires an increase to the baking time.

**Are there any special tricks to having a slightly uncooked center on purpose?**

Inserting a Hershey's Kiss or a dollop of cream cheese type filling (see the recipe in the recipe section) halfway through the baking time will give the feel of a softly

These ingredients also retain moisture very well.

cooked center. You can also create a soft center by using a recipe that contains a lot of fat, such as blondies or fudge brownies that also produce a moist center. Undercooking the cupcakes will also, but it isn't recommended.

**How do you know how much batter to put into the paper liners? I always seem to have too much (and the cupcakes look like mushrooms) or too little and the cupcakes are flat. What can I do to prevent this?**

For cupcakes that will not be stuffed, fill the well two-thirds full. For cupcakes that will be stuffed, fill them halfway. To ensure each well gets the same amount of batter, use a measuring cup to scoop the filling out of the bowl and into the well.

**If you're adapting a cake recipe, what do you change (time, temperature, ingredients)?**

Almost all cake recipes can be converted to cupcakes with very little trouble. The only element that needs to be changed is the time. They will usually bake in about 2/3 the time of a regular cake. For example, if a cake bakes for 35 minutes, the cupcakes will be done in about 22.

**Why doesn't the frosting stay on the cupcake when I frost it?**

One of the major reasons frosting doesn't 'stick' or stay on top is that the tops of the cupcakes are too moist. Let the cakes cool completely before frosting. If you will be storing them unfrosted, loosely cover the tops; otherwise, they will get sticky. A trick that some pastry chefs use is to spread a thin layer of frosting over the cupcake first, to seal in any crumbs and make a smooth surface. Then they frost as usual.

Another reason the frosting may not be sticking may be because the tops are oily. This is due to improper baking or storage (if the plastic wrap is pressing directly against the top of the cupcake, for example). Baking and storing cupcakes correctly should eliminate this problem.

**What is the secret to getting the perfect spongy texture?**

There are three secrets to getting the perfect cupcake texture: first, use the freshest ingredients, of the best quality available; second, follow the recipe, taking care especially to beat enough air into the batter or eggs, depending on which type of cake you are making (butter based or egg-white based); and third, bake it at the proper temperature until it is done, but not overbaked.

**What would be the best toppings for a banana cupcake?**

Cream cheese frosting would be excellent. Caramel frosting or a simple Buttercream spiked with cinnamon would also be a good choice. Try sprinkling a little nutmeg on top of the frosted cupcake.

If at all possible, try not to fill the cupcakes more than 1 or 2 days in advance.

**What is the best way to fill cupcakes with cream without cutting into them?**

Make the pastry bag do all the work with this easy method: Insert the tip of the pastry bag into the top or the bottom of the cupcake and squeeze gently while slowly lifting until filling is level with the top (or bottom) of the cupcake. If you insert the tip through the top of the cupcake you can finish frosting by moving the pastry bag in a circular motion while continuing to squeeze gently.

**What is the best way to get the pudding on the inside?**

Use the filling method described in the question above "What is the best way to fill cupcakes with cream without cutting into them?"

**How do you fill cupcakes without having them get soggy?**

If you are using fruit or jam, make sure that the filling is very well drained. Light fillings, like Cool Whip, leach much less moisture than heavy fillings like pudding. If at all possible, try not to fill the cupcakes more than 1 or 2 days in advance.

**About how long do cupcakes stay fresh? Are there any tips/secrets to keep them fresher longer?**

First, cool the cupcakes completely before frosting, covering, or storing. Cover unfrosted cupcakes loosely so that the tops stay dry. Unfrosted cupcakes will stay fresh up to five days in the fridge. Cupcakes, properly wrapped or stored, will stay fresh for three days on the countertop. Refrigerate cupcakes that are frosted with whipped cream or have creamy fillings. Frosted cupcakes may be refrigerated for three days. (Beyond these given times the texture starts to decline.)

For extra-long storage, store cupcakes in the freezer. They will stay fresh up to three months wrapped in plastic wrap inside an airtight container. It is best to freeze the frosting separately and decorate the cakes later, but as long as you don't use anything that will discolor the frosting while it thaws, fully-frosted cupcakes may also be frozen.

**How can I tell if my cupcakes are ready? Is there a way to test for doneness?**

Stick a toothpick in the center of the cupcake. If it comes out moist but clean, the cupcake is done. (A few crumbs are okay.) If it has batter clinging to it, the cupcakes need some more baking time. If it comes out very dry, the cupcakes are probably overbaked.

**What are the best ways to use fresh fruit in cupcakes?**

Cut up the fruit into small chunks and toss them with enough flour to coat the pieces evenly. This is to keep the fruit from becoming heavy and falling to the bottom of the cupcake. It also prevents the cupcakes from absorbing too much moisture and getting soggy.

If you notice that your cupcakes are coming out brown on the top, your oven might be running too hot.

**Can I substitute soymilk for milk or water in my cupcakes?**

Yes. You can substitute it using a 1:1 ratio, and no other adjustments to the recipe are needed. Some bakers swear by substituting 7-UP for milk for the moistness factor it adds.

**What is the correct temperature to bake the cupcakes?**

Follow the temperature detailed in the recipe. If you are inventing your own recipe, start with 350°F, 177°C or the temperature used to bake recipes containing similar ingredients. Always bake cupcakes in the middle of a pre-heated oven. If you notice that your cupcakes are coming out brown on the top, your oven might be running too hot. Try decreasing the temperature in increments of 25°F (14°C) for each batch until the cakes do not overbake. If the cakes are taking much longer to bake than the recipe says, your oven is probably too cold. Increase the temperature by 25°F, 14°C per batch until the cakes bake correctly.

**Why do my cupcakes have little tunnels in them?**

Under mixing can cause too few or uneven air pockets or bubbles in the mixture. As the sugar and butter are mixed and the sugar cuts into the butter, it forms air bubbles and the mixture becomes fluffy. Cut the mixing too short and the air bubbles are fewer, larger and less even.

Too much leavening and over mixing can cause the air bubbles to collapse in the structure of the batter, resulting in the tunneling effect as the structure is baked. Also, make sure to bake the cupcakes at the proper temperature, since an oven that is too hot can cause texture faults like this.

### How do you keep your cupcakes from deflating in the middle while baking?

The eggs must be of a good quality and fresh, as should the baking powder. Eggs that are old will not firm up as consistently as fresh eggs, resulting in cake that could be too soft or too tough. Baking powder that is too old will not leaven the batter enough.

It is also very important to follow the temperature and time guidelines in the recipe. Underbaking will cause the cakes to deflate when they are removed from the oven, and sometimes it is not apparent until they have cooled down. Also, the oven must not be too warm or the cakes will rise too quickly and collapse.

Also, the oven must not be too warm or the cakes will rise too quickly and collapse.

### How do you get the sprinkles to stick to the icing?

An easy trick is to pour the sprinkles into a wide, shallow container like a soup plate. Roll the frosted part of the cupcake gently but firmly in the sprinkles right after you frost it, and then give it a little shake. The loose sprinkles will fall off, but the rest will stay in place.

### How do you get nice domed cupcakes instead of ones that fall flat?

First, fill each well about 2/3 of the way. Any more than this and the cupcakes get unmanageable 'mushroom tops'; any less, and they will not rise above the rim of the liner. Make sure to use the recommended amount of leavening (baking soda or baking powder usually). Then, check the oven temperature. Finally, make sure to let them completely bake before taking them out of the oven. If the proteins in the eggs have not fully coagulated, the cupcakes will fall. You should try to keep the oven door closed until the minimum baking time has elapsed.

**How do you get cupcakes to form even, round tops, without spilling over the edges of the pan?**

Take care not to overfill the wells. Also, make sure to measure all ingredients accurately: Too much baking powder or baking soda can cause the cupcakes to rise too much. It can lead to a bitter or acrid flavor, too.

If some cupcakes are fine but others are flat, or if you notice them sloping, your oven is probably not level. Fix this by rotating the pan or pans, turning them front to back halfway through baking. (An exception to the recommendation is that you leave the oven door shut until the minimum baking time has elapsed.)

If the recipe says to bake for 20 minutes, set a timer to turn the cupcakes at the 10-12 minute mark. Be certain not to turn the pan before the halfway mark or your cupcakes could sink or collapse during the cooling phase.

**How much batter do you put in each cupcake liner, and how do I get the perfect amount of batter into each cup?**

Fill plain (i.e., unstuffed) cupcakes two-thirds of the way full. You can use a spring release ice cream scoop to measure out the right amount for each well. Alternately, if you have a turkey baster or similar tool with measuring lines along the side, use that. Don't just eyeball the amount.

**How can I alter an existing recipe for high level baking? Every time I try to make my cupcakes, they fall because of the altitude (7500 ft).**

Because atmospheric pressure is lower in high altitudes, the chemistry involved in cooking, especially baking, changes. Box mixes often have high-altitude instructions printed on the back or side of the box. You should follow those for each specific box mix. Otherwise you can follow the guidelines in the high altitude baking section.

**Is it okay to use special types of cake mix (even if it's from scratch), such as lemon or coconut cake batter, to make cupcakes? Or are there different batters that should be used only for cupcakes?**

Almost any batter would make good cupcakes. Extra care should be taken for angel food and chiffon type mixes: Never use greased cupcake wells or liners with these two types. Use paper or foil liners only, since anything oily will disrupt the egg whites and keep them from rising.

**Where can I find different types of sprinkles (different colors, textures, etc.) online? Is there a good online sprinkles site?**

Amazon.com offers many varieties of sprinkles, starting at $1.29 plus shipping. Baking giant Wilton.com offers 216 options, from colored sugars to sprinkle assortments to jumbo-sized sprinkles. Also check out the reading and resources section at the back of this book for additional resources.

**How much should I fill the cupcake wells in the pan?**

Fill plain (i.e., unstuffed) cupcakes two-thirds of the way. For cupcakes that are to be stuffed, fill halfway. The addition of the stuffing will make it up to two-thirds.

**How do I make those beautiful rosettes that you can make with different colored frostings? Is there a handy how-to anywhere?**

Wilton.com offers three pages worth of various icing decorations, including not only roses, but people, animals, and all types of flowers. The topic 'roses' (http://www.wilton.com/technique/Roses) comes with step-by-step instructions, pictures, and a how-to video.

**What can I add/take out of my cupcakes to make them fluffier? No matter which recipe or box mix I use, my cupcakes always come out with inverted dome tops.**

If this is happening, regardless of the recipe or mix you use, it could be two things: 1. Is your oven accurate?

If the cupcakes are being underbaked, they will fall as they cool, resulting in the inverted domes you describe.

2. Is your leavening agent (i.e., baking powder) fresh? Baking powder reacts to moisture and loses its strength over time.  It should be replaced every 3-6 months.

Make sure to follow the recipe exactly rather than substituting ingredients until you identify the issue causing this problem.

**How can I make cupcakes that taste good but that would be for a person with diabetes?**

Use agave nectar instead of sugar.  It is sweet, but it doesn't spike blood sugar. Use ½ - 2/3 cup (119 – 158 ml) agave syrup to one cup sugar if you are making cupcakes for sugar sensitive cupcake fans instead of the ¾ cup. Reduce any liquids accordingly about ¼ cup (59 ml) less liquid per cup (237 ml) of agave and bake at 25°F, 14°C lower than the stated temperature. Remember, substitution success will depend on the type of recipe you are using and you should always experiment with substitutions when the pressure is not on to create a masterpiece for a special event.

**Where is the best place to purchase decorations? The supermarket has a limited supply of interesting things.**

Amazon.com and Wilton.com are affordable and ever-popular, thanks to a wide selection.  For professionals, PastryChef.com's stock, while limited, is very useful. At the

If you are willing to experiment, this can be an ideal solution if you are looking to replace refined sugar in the recipe.

higher end of the price scale, Sur la Table offers unusual and gourmet items. See the Reading and Resources section at the back of this book for more great resources.

**What substitutes can you use for sugar to still give cupcakes a moist, sweet taste? I've tried applesauce but I never seem to get it right.**

Honey is hygroscopic; it draws in water and holds on to it. For small amounts, substitute it directly for sugar; in large amounts, use ¾ cup (178 ml) of honey to every cup (201 g) of sugar. Reduce liquids by ¼ cup (59 ml) per cup of honey. The cake will be denser and heavier than normal. Since honey browns slightly more quickly than sugar, it is advisable to reduce the oven temperature by 25°F, 14°C.

Agave nectar is also hygroscopic. Use 1/2-2/3 cup (191-158 ml) agave nectar for every cup of sugar (201 g). You should also reduce the oven temperature by 25°F, 14°C.

Even better, you can also use half applesauce or other fruit puree and half honey (or half agave). If you are willing to experiment, this can be an ideal solution if you are looking to replace refined sugar in the recipe. It will increase the moisture factor and you will be using less processed material.

If you use agave with a fruit puree from your own food processor, you can make a natural sugar substitute mixture that won't shoot your insulin levels up.

**How long should cupcakes sit in the pan before you take them out?**

Cupcakes should be removed from the pan within the first 3-5 minutes out of the oven.  A cooling rack is the best choice.  It allows air to circulate and keeps the bottoms from getting soggy.  If you use cupcake liners, removing the cupcakes onto a cooling rack will keep the liners from separating from the cupcakes.

If you are worried about burning your fingers or if you are not able to grab the crown of the cupcakes to transfer them quickly to the cooling rack safely, you can also use two toothpicks to remove the cupcakes from the pan.  Poke the first toothpick into the cupcake you want to remove at a 60 degree angle, and poke the other toothpick vertically on the opposite side in the opposite 60 degree angle and lift onto the cooling rack.

**What is a good frosting tip so the cupcakes look nice?**

Use the star or leaf tip that comes in a basic pastry bag kit.  They make professional-looking ridges and swirls as the frosting is applied.  No pastry bag?  Use a Ziploc bag with a ½ inch corner cut out to squeeze frosting out in a circular dollop on top.  It gives the same effect many cupcake bakeries use.  (See the technique discussed in "What is the easiest way to frost cupcakes?" – the next question.)

If you are worried about burning your fingers or if you are not able to grab the crown of the cupcakes to transfer them quickly to the cooling rack safely, you can also use two toothpicks to remove the cupcakes from the pan.

**What is the easiest way to frost cupcakes?**

For a thin, smooth layer of frosting, warm the frosting slightly, 10 or 15 seconds in the microwave, and stir it. Next, simply turn the cupcake upside down, placing the top into the bowl of frosting. Give it a twist and pull it out as you complete the second twist. The cupcake will have a simple, slender layer of frosting, with no mess or fuss.

For a greater amount of frosting, use a pastry bag or pastry gun with a wide star tip. Starting from the center, apply the frosting to the cake in circular motions until the base layer is covered. Continue spiraling upward while moving inward, like a soft-serve ice cream cone, until the desired amount of frosting is applied.

**If you add miniature candy bars to the poured batter, does it affect the baking time?**

It does not affect the baking time very much. You will probably need to add a minute onto the bake time to compensate for opening the oven. The best way to keep the bars suspended in the batter is to partially bake the cake until it is wobbly but starting to set – about 12 minutes. Then insert the candy into the cupcake and bake for 10 more minutes or until done. This is also the technique for inserting truffles into the center.

If you do not use cupcake liners, another way to insert miniature candy bars is to open a slit in the top of the cupcake right after you transfer the cupcakes from the oven to the cooling rack. They will melt and infuse chocolate into the center of the cupcake. You can hide the slit when you frost the top. It's also easy to insert a Hershey Kiss upside down into a cupcake this way.

**What are some different things you can bake cupcakes in besides cupcake pans, and paper cups?**

Cupcakes were originally baked in ramekins and teacups.  If you have teacups that will stand up to the heat of the oven, spray them lightly and dust them with powdered sugar then fill them about halfway with batter (for a neat, rounded top about even with the rim).  There is a wide variety of ramekins available today in a variety of sizes.  These are perfect for baking cupcakes for an elegant occasion, including a formal dinner party.

Start baking as directed, but depending on the size of your teacup or ramekin, they may need a longer time in the oven than a regular cupcake.  Use a toothpick or cake tester to test for doneness. A cupcake that is finished baking will reveal a clean toothpick or cake tester after insertion and removal.

Some cooks like the easy clean up of Silicone liners. If you want to use these to bake cupcakes outside of a traditional cupcake pan, make sure to use the thickest ones available.  The thinner versions will collapse.

You can also use party nut cups. They are plain white sturdy food service cups with more substance than cupcake liners. You can even get them in different colors now. You can place these party nut cups filled with cupcake batter directly on a cookie sheet and put them straight into the oven. Using this technique can allow you to bake more cupcakes per batch, plus these cups come in standard and mini sizes. You can get them on Amazon.com.

**How do you flavor the frosting perfectly so it's not too sweet?**

Instead of a simple buttercream, which relies heavily on powdered sugar, try a Golden Buttercream, which uses a small quantity of corn starch (or arrowroot powder) to reduce sugar, or an Italian Buttercream, which relies on eggs for consistency.

Cream cheese and whipped cream frostings are also less sweet. One of my favorites is a cream cheese frosting. I personally use low fat or fat free cream cheese (and sometimes soy cream cheese) with pure vanilla extract and a teaspoon (5 ml) of lime (citrus fruit) zest sweetened with agave nectar. It is a healthier substitute that allows me to eat cupcakes with less guilt!

If it is not hot outside and you are willing to frost the cupcakes right before serving, a really low fat option is to drain your favorite plain low fat yogurt overnight in a sieve. The yogurt is then thicker. You can whip it up with a ¼ agave nectar and 1 tsp. (5 ml) of real vanilla extract. Citrus zest, coconut shreds and bits of fresh fruit makes this a fresh and healthy option instead of frosting if you're looking for a substitute.

**Is it necessary to spray the cupcake liners with a non-stick spray?**

Not usually. You might consider it for butter-based cupcakes if sticking is a problem, but do not spray the

You can whip it up with a ¼ agave nectar and 1 tsp. (5 ml) of real vanilla extract.

liners if you are making angel food or chiffon cupcakes.

Can I substitute butter for shortening if the recipe calls for shortening?

Yes. Butter is actually a better choice than shortening because of its flavor and mouth feel. Use the same amount of butter as shortening.

If you are vegan or want to avoid dairy, there are new non-hydrogenated vegetable shortenings. Check your local health food store. Whole Foods always has it in stock.

**Does the order I mix the ingredients in matter?**

Yes, in most cases it does. When you are following a recipe it is very important to follow the mixing directions exactly. Many complex chemical reactions occur in baking, even in the mixing process. Unless the ingredients are added as instructed, the correct reaction may be disrupted and disappointing cupcakes can easily be the consequence.

**What is the best type of pan to use: dark, light, aluminum, cast iron or another type?**

Most cupcake recipes are based on using standard non-stick muffin pans. Darker-colored pans may heat up faster, and overbrown the bottoms, so check them about five minutes before the timer goes off just to ensure that the cupcakes aren't getting overbaked. Glass pans that have been tempered to take the heat of the oven are acceptable if the cupcakes are removed immediately after baking. Aluminum pans are a good choice if you use cupcake liners. However, aluminum pans can react with some batters leaching a metallic taste into the cupcakes. Older aluminum pans can develop hot spots, so you may want to avoid using older pans. Both aluminum pans and cast iron pans are reactive; acidic ingredients react with the metals and flavor the cupcakes in undesirable ways. Use cupcake liners to avoid the problem.

My favorite is to use the standard aluminum muffin tins with either plain paper cupcake liners or parchment paper liners. I also love using party nut cups on a cookie sheet.

**What is the craziest thing that can be accomplished when making a cupcake?**

Cupcakes have been dressed up, disguised as animals, shipped across continents, stuffed, filled with cream, shoved in ice cream cones, miniaturized, super-sized, and topped with everything imaginable. The craziest thing that can be done with making cupcakes is whatever crazy thing your imagination comes up with. (By the way, according to the Guardian's website (guardian.co.uk), the world's largest cupcake weighed in at 150 kg/330.6 lbs and stood 1.2m/3.9 ft tall. It reportedly fed 2,000 people. There is some controversy whether this counts as the world's official largest, since it is not one 'solid' piece but was baked in pieces.)

**How do you make cupcakes in an ice cream cone without burning the cone?**

Some cooks recommend covering the cones in tin foil to help them stay upright and to protect them from burning; others recommend rotating the pan and adjusting the cones 2-3 times during baking. An easier idea is to bake the cupcakes as usual and, when they have cooled, trim the sides and bottom of the cupcakes to fit the cones. Use a bit of frosting to anchor the bottom of the cupcake to the cone, and make sure the fit is snug. Frost as described below. Use regular cupcakes for the standard ice cream cones. Mini cupcakes fit nicely in the sugar cones.

**How do you make cupcake cones with frosting?**

Fit the cupcake into the cone and use a pastry bag to apply the frosting.

**How long should I wait to frost a cupcake after it comes out of the oven? Would it be okay to frost the cupcakes after they have sat overnight or after they have been refrigerated?**

Cupcakes must be completely cool before frosting, or else the frosting will melt. It is fine to frost them at any time if they have been properly stored; in fact, it is best to frost them the day they will be served. If the cupcakes have been refrigerated, let them get to room temperature before you frost them to avoid any problems with condensation and excess moisture. If you

If you frost a cupcake before bringing it to room temperature then moisture can form between the cupcake and the frosting and the frosting can slide off.

frost a cupcake before bringing it to room temperature, moisture can form between the cupcake and the frosting and the frosting can slide off.

**What can I use in place of egg to make cupcakes for a child allergic to eggs?**

Many egg substitutes are readily available online and at grocery stores. They use wheat, rice, or soy protein to replace the protein in the egg. Follow the recommendations on the package. (Available online at amazon.com and ener-g.com.) You can also refer to the egg substitute chart on page 119 for additional ideas.

**What is the best product to use to keep the cupcakes from sticking to the baking pan? Some products change the taste, and not for the better.**

The easiest alternative is to use a light-tasting flour baking spray. If you are not gluten intolerant, then the baking sprays combined with flour coat the best. The best-tasting alternative is to rub a light coating of pure butter or coconut oil into the cupcake wells, gently wipe with a paper towel, then apply a dusting of powdered sugar. This is my favorite non-gluten way when I'm not using cupcake liners.

**Can I make cupcakes with olive oil? I made cookies with olive oil and they tasted fantastic and were probably a little bit healthier than butter.**

Yes. Some boxed recipes call for oil instead of butter; just substitute an equal amount of coconut oil or light olive oil.  For butter-based cakes, use 2/3 cup (158 ml) olive oil (or coconut oil) per cup (227 g) of butter or shortening.  To avoid a heavy olive taste, make sure to use a light-tasting type of olive oil. You still will taste a difference. Be sure to experiment with this substitution outside of a big event, birthday, or other occasion where the taste difference might be unacceptable and prove to be a disaster. Depending on the olive oil and recipe, this can ruin the taste of some cupcakes in most people's opinion. The easiest cupcakes in which to use olive oil are cupcake recipes that include semi-sweet chocolate as an ingredient; otherwise, use virgin coconut oil, which is my favorite.

**What is a good substitute for butter if you are allergic or opposed to eating dairy?**

Coconut oil is excellent cooking oil for vegans or those allergic to dairy.  It has a unique, almost tropical taste, and unlike artificial shortenings, it melts in the mouth.  Subtract ¼ cup (59 ml) of liquid from the recipe to compensate for the difference in texture. You can also find vegan non-hydrogenated shortenings on the market now.

**How do you keep the tops or bottoms of cupcakes from browning before the cupcakes are done in the middle?**

The cupcake pan should be placed in the center of the oven. Placed too close to the top, the cupcakes will burn on top.  Also, check to be sure your oven is not 'running hot'

Reduce the oven temperature by 25°F, 14°C when using honey or agave or similar syrup as a sweetener.

Consider using a baking spray with flour to ensure ease of release, or a baking oil spray dusted with powdered sugar.

or baking at a higher temperature than it indicates. (Use an oven thermometer to do this.) Another possible cause is too much sugar in the recipe. If excessive browning continues, try covering the cupcakes with aluminum foil for the last 5-7 minutes of baking.

**Note:** Cupcakes made with honey, agave and similar viscosity tend to brown faster than cupcakes made with sugar. Reduce the oven temperature by 25°F, 14°C when using honey or agave or similar syrup as a sweetener.

### How well do the "flexible" Silicone cupcake cups and pans work?

Reviews are mixed. Most users are happy with the flexible Silicone cupcake cups' non-stick properties, although some bakers note it is harder to free the cupcakes in the middle of the pan. More than one baker has complained about the plastic-like smell that cheaper Silicone pans and cups give off when they are heated. The more expensive models generally performed better. Is the non-stickiness worth the extra price tag? It depends who you ask.

**Note:** Cheaper versions of Silicone bakeware are not always 100% Silicone. They may contain some plastic. Research each brand carefully before buying. Consider using a baking spray with flour to ensure ease of release, or a baking oil spray dusted with powdered sugar.

**Is there any time when frosting/decorating must be completed when the cupcakes are hot?**

Even toppings like Ganache and flavor infusions are usually added when the cupcakes have cooled. Too much heat may cause the frosting to start to seep into the cupcake. If that is the effect you're going for, then go ahead and experiment. Use a pastry brush to control how much you use, so the cupcakes don't turn into mush.

**How can I prevent chocolate chips, fruit, etc., from falling right to the bottom of the cupcake when baking?**

Coat cupcake mix-ins with a small amount of flour or powdered sugar, then add them into the batter right before baking to keep them from sinking to the bottom. Chocolate chips may be pressed into a partially-baked cupcake.

**Are there better boxed-cake mixes for cupcakes vs. cakes?**

The back of the box will tell you. Most cake mixes can be easily converted into cupcakes; in fact, there are almost always directions on the back or side of the box telling you how to do so. If the manufacturers of the cake mix don't recommend making cupcakes with their product, look elsewhere.

Coat cupcake mix-ins with a small amount of flour or powdered sugar, then add them into the batter right before baking to keep them from sinking to the bottom.

**How do you make cupcakes that are light and fluffy rather than heavy and dense?**

The lightest, fluffiest cupcakes are a result of more air bubbles (that have not popped) being expanded and sealed by the heated during the baking process. Chemical leaveners like baking soda and baking powder do not add air bubbles. They only expand the ones already there.

Too much leavening will cause overexpansion and popping of the bubbles. Either way, the end result is not enough bubbles baked into the final cupcakes. Always check to ensure you are incorporating enough air and the correct amount of leavening.

You can also try something new. Instead of relying on a traditional butter-based recipe, try using sponge cake or angel food cake recipes. These rely on whipped eggs whites instead of butter, so the overall product is lighter and fluffier due to all the extra air incorporated into the batter via the egg whites. They tend to be lower in fat and calories, too!

**I love cupcakes with loads of frosting, but they tend to be messy to eat. How can I frost the cupcakes without getting frosting on the top of the wrapper?**

Use a pastry bag fitted with a decorative tip to neatly pipe the frosting on top of the cupcake, avoiding the edge. For additional protection, you can cut thin strips of wax paper and place them over the rim of the cupcake while it is being frosted. Remove them when you have finished frosting. If you want extra frosting, you can also insert the pastry bag tip into the top or the underside of the cupcake and add some frosting inside before you frost the top.

**Do you recommend allowing the cupcakes to be taken out earlier than suggested and having them sit for a time after baking?**

No. Allow them to cook thoroughly, and then remove them from the oven. Take them out of the pan within the first 3-5 minutes after you take them out of the oven and allow them to cool. Undercooking can present a host of problems: a coarse or soggy texture; cupcakes that fall after removing them from the oven; uncooked centers and more (include the dangers of undercooked eggs).

**What is the best way to make molten chocolate cupcakes?**

Using the partially baked method, press an unshelled chocolate truffle into a cupcake removed from the oven approximately 12 minutes into the baking time. Do not open the oven door until the halfway mark or your cupcakes can fall. Once you insert the truffle, return the cupcake to the oven to finish baking. You may need to add a minute or two to the bake time depending on how long the oven door is open.

If you don't have time to make your own homemade truffles, I love to use Lindor® truffles. Simply remove the wrapper (if you are using a wrapped truffle) and insert it into the half-baked cupcake. Finish baking. Allow the cupcakes to cool briefly, but serve them while they are still quite warm. The molten chocolate center will ooze out. (If no chocolate truffles are available, scoop out scant soup spoonfuls of Ganache that has been allowed to set. Roll them into balls. Freeze them. And use in place of the truffle.) You can even make Ganache balls in batches and freeze them so you have them handy whenever the mood strikes.

**How do I make cupcakes stay firm and not fall apart without using baking cups?**

Be sure to lightly grease or butter each well and sugar the bottom and sides with confectioner's (powdered) sugar. Use a paper towel to lightly coat each cupcake well in the pan and sprinkle the sugar around the bottom and sides of each well. Hold the pan upside down and tap it to get rid of any excess sugar. Bake as usual. When the pan comes out of the oven, remove each cupcake (a fork will be helpful) and cool on a rack.

**Note:** Angel food or chiffon cupcakes need special handling. Consult the box mix or recipe you are using for details.

**How are upside down cupcakes made?**

A few spoonfuls of topping are placed in the bottom of the cupcake liner, then the batter is added on top. You can use a pineapple upside down cake and make it into cupcakes by adjusting the baking time by about half. You can also put granola, dried or fresh fruit slices, nuts, dates, raisons, Oreo cookie pieces or a mixture of whatever your imagination can come up with.

**Is it possible to use the microwave to make cupcakes? If so, what changes should be made to a recipe?**

It is possible, but not necessarily advisable. Microwaves cook by agitating water molecules to create heat, so it really is an entirely different ball game. Baking in a microwave is a tricky job due to hotspots and other anomalies that don't usually happen or can be isolated and avoided in a conventional oven. That being said, several recipes are available for microwaved cupcakes that are based on box mixes, soda pop, and occasionally yogurt.

**Can you add a spice to your cupcake batter to make it taste totally different, but still good, and if so what spice?**

Cinnamon is ever-popular and a delicious addition to vanilla, chocolate, caramel and apple cakes. A few teaspoons/mililiter will totally change any recipe, and no other alterations are needed. Some other ideas to spice up vanilla cakes are apple pie spice, allspice, anise, or grated citrus peel. A teaspoon (1.67 g) of Espresso powder will pump up the chocolatey goodness of any chocolate cupcake recipe.

# Part 10

## RECIPES

# Basic Vanilla Buttermilk Cupcake Recipe

1 cup butter (227 grams)
2 cups sugar (402 grams)
1 Tbsp. (15 ml) white vinegar or lemon juice (fresh if possible)
1 cup less 1 Tbsp./ (222 ml) milk
4 large eggs
2 teaspoons (10 ml) real vanilla extract
3 1/4 cups (339 g) cake flour
2 teaspoons (10 ml) of baking powder

**Preparation:**
1. Preheat oven to 350°F, 177°C.
2. Take the eggs, milk and butter out of the refrigerator.
3. Add 1 Tbsp. (15 ml) of white vinegar or lemon juice into a cup/liquid measure, pour milk into the cup measure to finish filling. Put the milk back in the refrigerator.
4. Separate the eggs; yolks in one bowl, egg whites in another.
5. Measure the butter, and cut the butter into Tbsp. (14.18 g) size chunks.
6. Let the one cup (237 ml) milk/vinegar mixture, the butter and eggs sit out at room temperature for 1/2 hour before adding into the batter.
7. Pull out the remaining ingredients from storage and place on the counter.
8. Coat and/or line the cupcake tins.

### Mixing the Batter

Stir the flour and measure it by spooning the flour into the measuring cup and pour into a bowl. Measure and add the baking powder into the bowl with the flour. Mix the baking powder into the flour, then sift the flour and baking powder into another clean bowl.

In a mixing bowl, blend the butter and sugar on high with a hand mixer (or stand mixer) until they are creamed together and form a very pale yellow mixture that is light, fluffy and the sugar granules are dissolved into the butter. Beat the egg yolks into the creamed butter-sugar mixture. Then mix in the milk and vanilla.

Add the flour-baking powder mixture 1/2 cup (119 ml) at a time by sprinkling each 1/2 cup (119 ml) into the batter, mix in the flour on low speed. Sprinkle the next 1/2 and repeat this process until all the flour is combined.

Next, using your stand or hand mixer, beat the egg whites from your separated eggs until stiff peaks form. Stir 1/4 of the beaten egg whites into the batter with a wooden spoon, then carefully fold the rest into the batter. Fold the remaining egg whites into the batter and stir just enough to get the batter mixed.

Fill the cupcake wells. Bake for 20 minutes, remove from oven and remove the cupcakes onto a cooling rack. Let cool for 1 hour before frosting.

# Basic Gluten-Free Vanilla Buttermilk Cupcake Recipe

Why I love this recipe: This Gluten Free powerhouse tastes so good that the cupcakes are rarely around long enough to frost. The recipe uses sugar substitute Purevia® and date sugar. The flavor of the date sugar adds a lovely natural sweet flavor and a lovely browning.

½ cup butter (113.4 grams)
½ cup organic virgin coconut oil (104 grams)
1 cup date sugar (192 grams)
24 stick packets of Purevia® (equivalent to 1 cup sugar)
1 Tbsp. (15 ml) white vinegar or lemon juice (fresh if possible)
1 cup less 1 Tbsp./ (222 ml) Silk® soy milk
4 large eggs, separated
2 teaspoons (10 ml) real vanilla extract

Flour Mixture:
1 cup Bob's Red Mill® Brown Rice Flour
1 cup Bob's Red Mill® Tapioca Flour
1 cup Bob's Red Mill® Sorghum Flour
2 teaspoons (10 ml) of baking powder

**Preparation:**

1. Preheat oven to 350°F, 177°C or your convection oven to 325°F, 162.8°C.
2. Take the eggs, milk and butter out of the refrigerator.
3. Add 1 Tbsp. (15 ml) of white vinegar or lemon juice into a cup/liquid measure, pour the soy milk into the cup, measure to finish filling. Put the milk back in the refrigerator.
4. Separate the eggs; yolks in one bowl, egg whites in another.
5. Measure the butter, and cut the butter into Tbsp. (15 g) size chunks.
6. Let the one cup (237 ml) milk/vinegar mixture, the butter and eggs sit out at room temperature for 1/2 hour before adding into the batter.
7. Pull out the remaining ingredients from storage and place on the counter.
8. Coat and/or line the cupcake tins.
9. Bare Bottomed Cupcakes: This recipe does very well without cupcake liners. Coat the cupcake wells with a paper towel dipped in the coconut oil. Dust with powdered sugar and shake the excess off.
10. Foil liners: If you do use cupcake liners, using foil liners will keep the cupcakes from getting as browned as with the other methods. Also, the tops of the cupcakes may crack while baking. Doesn't affect the flavor and it can easily be covered with frosting.

    Paper liners: If you use paper liners, the coconut oil will make them greasy. Again, no affect on the flavor and they do keep longer, but then again they probably won't be around long enough to need a paper liner to keep them from drying out.

**Mixing the Batter**

Prepare the Flour Mixture:

Measure the gluten-free flours by spooning a cup of each flour into the measuring cup and pour into a medium bowl. Measure and add the baking powder into the bowl with the flour. Stir all the flours together with a wire whip and mix the baking powder into the flour. Sift the flour and baking powder mixture into another clean bowl. This is important in order to incorporate as much air into the flours as possible.

Combine the Wet Ingredients:

In a mixing bowl, blend the butter, coconut oil on high with a hand mixer (or stand mixer) until they are creamed together (about 30 seconds if at room temperature as required) and form a pale yellow mixture that is light, fluffy. Add the date sugar and Purevia® and mix on medium for 1 ½ minutes. The mixture will be brownish and the date sugar granules will not be dissolved into the butter. Let this mixture sit for 15 minutes.

After the butter/sugar mixture has set for 15 minutes, beat the egg yolks into the creamed butter-sugar mixture. Then mix in the soy buttermilk mixture and vanilla.

Add the gluten free flour/baking powder mixture 1/2 cup (70 g) at a time by sprinkling each 1/2 cup (70 g) into the batter, mix in the flour on low speed. Sprinkle the next ½ cup (70 g) and repeat this process until all the flour mixture is combined.

Next, using your clean stand or hand mixer and a clean bowl, beat the egg whites from your separated eggs on medium until stiff peaks form. Stir 1/4 of the beaten egg whites into the batter with a wooden spoon, then carefully fold the rest into the batter. Fold the remaining egg whites into the batter and stir just enough to get the batter mixed. This is another key to adding enough air into the batter.

Fill the cupcake wells. Bake for 20 minutes for regular cupcakes, or 12 minutes for mini-cupcakes, remove from oven and remove the cupcakes onto a cooling rack. Let cool for 1 hour before frosting.

If your oven doesn't brown the cupcakes enough, you can turn on the broiler for 30 seconds to 1 minute and you can watch through the oven door as they get a touch brown. I love the browning I get with this recipe in my $79 Hamilton Beach Countertop Oven with Convection using the convection setting. It beats my full size oven baking cupcakes every day.

Nutritional Information Per Mini-Cupcake: 95 calories, 1.2 grams protein, 0.5 grams fiber.

# Simple Buttercream Frosting

2 cups (230 g) powdered sugar
1 tsp (5 ml) pure vanilla extract
¼ cup (57 g) unsalted butter, very soft
3 oz (88.7 ml) milk

Sift the powdered sugar. Beat the butter and sugar together until the mixture crumbs. Add the vanilla to the milk and pour into the sugar mixture. Beat until smooth. Frosting should be thick and creamy. Add more sugar or milk if the mixture is not exactly the consistency you desire.

### Flavored Versions of Simple Buttercream Frosting

**Chocolate:** Add 2 Tbsp. (10 g) cocoa powder and 1 tsp. (1.67 g) of instant espresso to the sugar.

**Coconut:** Substitute coconut milk for the milk or cream.

**Cream Cheese:** Substitute softened cream cheese for the butter.

**Golden Buttercream:** Simple buttercream prepared with melted butter. Substitute 2 Tbsp. (20 g) of cornstarch for ½ cup (57.5 g) of powdered sugar.

# Chocolate Mascarpone Filling

8 oz softened mascarpone (you can substitute cream cheese)
1 egg
1/3 c sugar
6 oz grated chocolate
1 tsp (5 ml) vanilla extract
¼ tsp. (1.5 g) sea salt

Cream the softened cream cheese and sugar until fluffy. Add in the room temperature egg (or pasteurized egg substitute), and vanilla. Blend thoroughly. Finally, mix in the grated chocolate and drop by the spoonful into cupcake batter in each unbaked cupcake well. Bake as directed. Fills 24 cupcakes.

**Note:** This filling will be very soft when uncooked. To make it easier to scoop out, allow to chill before using.

# Brown Sugar Buttercream (An Italian Buttercream)

3 large egg whites at room temperature
1/8 tsp. (.75 g) salt
1 cup (239 grams) packed dark brown sugar
1/2 cup (119 ml) water
1/2 tsp. (2.5 ml) fresh lemon juice
1-1/2 cups (3 sticks/339 g) unsalted butter, cut into pieces
　and softened
2 teaspoons (10 ml) vanilla
Special equipment:  a candy thermometer

1. Mix egg whites and salt in a large glass or metal bowl.
2. Bring the brown sugar and water to a boil over medium high heat in a small pan. Boil the mixture into a syrup. When the syrup reaches 238°F or 115°C as measured by the candy thermometer, remove from the heat and pour into a heat-tested glass measuring cup.
3. While the syrup is beginning to boil, beat the egg whites on medium high speed until bubbles begin to grow in volume. Add the lemon juice and continue mixing on medium speed until the egg whites form soft peaks. Set aside until the syrup above is ready.
4. Pour the syrup from the glass cup down the side of bowl containing the egg whites while mixing at high speed. Beat for about 6 minutes, scraping down the sides of the bowl with

a rubber spatula until the mixture is cool.

5. Add the butter one piece at a time (only once the egg mixture is completely cool) mixing it at medium speed after adding each piece. Add the vanilla and mix for an additional minute.

# Part 11

# APPENDICES

A.  Recipe Conversions
B.  Substitutions
C.  Cupcake Baking Terminology
D.  Checklists
E.  Calculating Calories and Points for Your Cupcakes
F.  Readings and Resources
G.  Online Tools

*Appendix A*

# Recipe Conversions

Google reports nearly 750,000 results available through their search for "cupcake recipe" results. It could take an entire lifetime to bake even 1%. It is more common than ever to run across a delicious sounding cupcake recipe on the Internet that uses unfamiliar measurements. Here are the secret formulas so you can convert anything.

### Converting to U.S. from Metric

- Grams to ounces: divide by 28.35
- Milliliters to fluid ounces: divide by 29.47
- Liters to quarts: divide by 0.946
- Kilograms to pounds: divide by 0.454

### Converting to Metric from U.S.

- Ounces to grams: multiply by 28.35
- Fluid Ounces to milliliters: multiply by 29.47
- Quarts to liters: multiply by 0.946
- Pounds to kilograms: multiply by 0.454

# Volume Measures Conversions

Metric equivalents are rounded.

| U.S. Measurement | Liquid Metric Measurement |
|---|---|
| ¼ tsp. | 1.25 milliliters |
| ½ tsp. | 2.5 milliliters |
| 1 tsp. | 5 milliliters |
| 1 Tbsp. | 15 milliliters |
| 1 fluid ounce/2 Tbsp. | 30 milliliters |
| 2 fluid ounces/4 Tbsp./1/4 cup | 59 milliliters |
| 8 fluid ounces/1 cup | 237 milliliters |
| 16 fluid ounces/2 cups/1 pint | 473 milliliters (0.48 liters) |
| 32 fluid ounces/2 pints/1 quart | 947 milliliters (0.95 liters) |
| 33.8 ounces | 1 liter |
| 128 fluid ounces/4 quarts/1 gallon | 3.75 liters |

## Volume Measurement Equivalents

| | | | | | | |
|---|---|---|---|---|---|---|
| 1 tsp. | | | 1/3 Tbsp. | 5 ml | | |
| 1 Tbsp. | 1/16th cup | ½ fluid ounce | 3 tsp. | 15 ml | | |
| 1 fluid ounce | | | 2 Tbsp. | 30 ml | | |
| 1 gill | ½ cup | 4 fluid ounces | 8 Tbsp. | 119 ml | | |
| ¼ cup | | 2 fluid ounces | 4 Tbsp. | 59 ml | | |
| ½ cup | | 4 fluid ounces | 8 Tbsp. | 119 ml | | |
| 1 cup | | 8 fluid ounces | 16 Tbsp. | 237 ml | | |
| 1 pint | 2 cups | 16 fluid ounces | 32 Tbsp. | 474ml | | |
| 1 quart | 4 cups | 32 fluid ounces | | 946 ml (.95 liters) | 2 pints | |
| 1 gallon | 16 cups | 128 fluid ounces | | 3.75 liters | 8 pints | 4 quarts |

## Key Fahrenheit To Celsius Equivalents
(rounded up)

| Fahrenheit | Celsius |
| --- | --- |
| 32° | 0° |
| 75° | 24° |
| 100° | 38° |
| 150° | 66° |
| 175° | 80° |
| 200° | 94° |
| 225° | 108° |
| 250° | 121° |
| 275° | 135° |
| 300° | 149° |
| 325° | 163° |
| 350° | 177° |
| 375° | 191° |
| 400° | 205° |
| 425° | 219° |
| 450° | 233° |

How to convert a temperature:
Equation to convert from Fahrenheit to Celsius:

$$C=(F-32) \times 5/9$$

Equation to convert Celsius to Fahrenheit:
$$F=(9/5 \times C) + 32$$

## Adjusting Cupcake Recipes for Humidity

If you are baking cupcakes in a humid climate, on a random humid day or during the thunderstorms of spring, you will have better results if you take these tips into account while you are choosing your recipe and frosting your cupcakes.

- Slightly decrease the amount of liquid in your recipe or slightly increase the amount of flour. This is because your flour and sugar will absorb moisture from the surrounding air. This is an area in which there are no hard or easy guidelines to pass along because the humidity from locale to locale varies greatly. Start out by asking your local resident expert bakers for guidance.

- Increase your mixing time slightly also. Remember not to get carried away so you don't overdevelop the gluten.

- Creaming butter and sugar successfully in humid weather can be tricky, as butter may not stick together smoothly, creating a lumpy batter with uneven air bubbles.

- Egg white-dependent recipes such as foam or sponge cake recipes made by whipping egg whites with sugar are tricky because the sugar attracts the moisture in the air. Save these kinds of cupcake recipes for dry days. Egg whites whipped up on a day too humid will be sticky or limp.

- Also, in colder, drier weather you may need to slightly increase the amount of liquid and decrease the amount of flour.

- Fluffy frostings dependent on whipping cream or eggs to give them volume, and frosting dependent on coconut oil or refrigerated ingredients will not perform well in humidity.

## Adjusting Cupcake Recipes for Altitude

The farther above sea level you get, the less heat (energy) it takes to turn water to steam. Steam is a powerful leavener. Liquids in the cupcake batter turn to steam and expand the air bubbles in the batter to expand the structure before the heat of the oven seals it.

High altitude baking is an art in itself. Cupcake recipes (and other baking recipes) are written for low altitudes and many times do not include instructions on how to adjust the recipe for higher elevations.

The adjustments listed here are suggested points to start with. Your adjustments may need your tweaking as changes in altitude and humidity factors vary from locale to locale even within communities.

An encyclopedia entry on high altitude baking could provide you with an exact combination for where you live. The perfect combination of change for your particular locale can be found only through experimentation. You can come close the first time. Start by making small adjustments first to see how it affects the outcome of your recipe.

Start by increasing the oven temperature and decrease the baking time according to the following guidelines. This combination can do the trick without anything else being needed. Of course, if you are following a recipe that includes high altitude baking instructions, follow those instructions particular to that recipe.

Here is a list of possible tweaks you may need to make:

- Increase the oven temperature 15°–25°F, 9°-11°C. Use the smaller end of adjustment for sponge or chocolate cake type recipes.
- Decrease the baking time by 16-26%.
- Reduce the sugar by 1 Tbsp. (12.56 g) per cup (201 g/7.1 oz).
- Increase the liquid in the recipe by 3-6 teaspoons (15-60 ml) for 3,000 feet above sea level. Add 1-½ tsp. (7.5 ml) for every additional 1,000 feet above 3,000 feet. Increasing the egg liquid in the recipe will add additional structure. For recipes that use egg whites for structure, increase the eggs as the liquid.
- Add 2-3 teaspoons (5-7.5 g) flour at 3,000 feet above sea level. Add 1 tsp. (2.5 g) for each additional 500 feet. The additional gluten provided in the flour adds support to the cupcake structure.

*Appendix B*

# Substitutions

## Miscellaneous Ingredient Substitutions

### Allspice
Amount: 1 tsp. (2.1 g)
Substitute: 1/2 tsp. (2.6 g) cinnamon plus 1/2 tsp. (1.1 g)
   ground cloves
OR 2/3 tsp. (3.47 g) cinnamon plus 1/3 tsp. (0.73 g)
   ground cloves

### Ammonium bicarbonate:
Amount: 3/4 tsp. (3 g)
Substitute: 1 tsp. (4 g) baking soda

### Apple Pie Spice
Amount: 1 tsp. (5 ml)
Substitute: 1/2 tsp. (2.6 g) cinnamon plus 1/4 tsp. (1.25 g)
   nutmeg plus 1/8 tsp. (0.3 g) cardamom

### Arrowroot starch
Amount: 1 tsp. (4.17 g)
Substitute: 1 Tbsp. (7.5 g) flour or
1-1/2 tsp. (5 g)  cornstarch

**Baking Powder, Double-Acting**

Amount: 1 tsp. (4 g)

Substitute: 1/4 tsp. (1 g) baking soda plus 5/8 tsp. (1.97 g) cream of tartar

OR 1/4 tsp. (1 g) baking soda plus 1/2 cup sour milk (119 ml) or buttermilk or yogurt (decrease liquid called for in recipe by 1/2 cup)

OR 1/4 tsp. (1 g) baking soda plus 1 1/2 Tbsp. (22.125 ml) vinegar or lemon juice used with sweet milk to make 1/2 cup (119 ml)   (decrease liquid called for in recipe by 1/2 cup)

OR 1/4 tsp. (1 g) baking soda plus 1/4 to 1/2 cup molasses (decrease liquid in recipe by 1 to 2 Tbsp./15-30 ml)

OR 1/3 tsp. (1.33 g) baking soda plus 1/2 tsp. (1.575 g) cream of tartar

**Baking Soda:**

1 teaspoon (4 g) baking soda - 2 tsp. (8 g) double-acting baking powder + replace acidic liquid ingredient in recipe with non-acidic liquid.  Or 3/4 tsp. (3 g) ammonium bicarbonate

**Baking Powder:**

Amount: Up to 12 tsp. or 4 Tbsp. (48 g)

Substitute: Sift together 2 Tbsp. (18.9 g) cream of tartar, plus
1 Tbsp. (12 g) baking soda, plus 1 Tbsp. (10 g) cornstarch.
1 tsp. (3.4 g) of this mix is equivalent to 1 tsp. (4 g) of
generic baking powder

**Buttermilk**

Amount: 1 cup (119 ml)

Substitute: 1 Tbsp. (15 ml) lemon juice or vinegar plus
enough regular milk to make 1 cup (119 ml) (allow to
stand 5 minutes)

**Chocolate chips**

Amount: 1 ounce (28.35 g)

Substitute: 1 ounce sweet cooking chocolate, semisweet

**Chocolate, Semisweet**

Amount: 1-2/3 ounces (47.25 g) semisweet

Substitute: 1 ounce unsweetened chocolate plus 4 tsp.
(16.75 g) sugar

**Chocolate, Semisweet**

Amount: 6 ounces (170.1 g) semisweet

Substitute: 2 squares unsweetened chocolate pieces, plus
2 Tbsp. (30 ml) shortening melted and 1/2 cup (100.5 g)
sugar

**Chocolate, Unsweetened**

Amount: 1 ounce (28.35 g)

Substitute: 3 Tbsp. (15 g) cocoa plus 1 Tbsp. (14.18 g) unsalted butter or coconut oil OR 3 Tbsp. (20 g) carob powder plus 2 Tbsp. (30 ml) of hot water

**Cocoa, (Unsweetened, Natural)** – acids are not neutralized

Amount: 1/4 cup (20.5 g)

Substitute: 1 ounce, or 1 square baking chocolate, and decrease the fat called for in recipe by 1½ teaspoons (1.18 g)

Amount: 3 Tbsp. (15 g)

3 Tbsp. (15 g) Dutch processed cocoa plus 1/8 tsp. (0.75 g) Cream of Tartar or 1/8 tsp. (0.6 ml) lemon juice or vinegar

**NOTE:** You cannot substitute Natural Cocoa for Dutch Processed cocoa without adjustment.

**Cocoa, Dutch Processed (Unsweetened, Alkalized)** – acids are neutralized.

Amount: 3 Tbsp. (15 g)

Substitute: 3 Tbsp. (15 g) natural cocoa powder plus pinch (1/8 tsp./0.75 g) baking soda

**Coconut**

Amount: 1 Tbsp. (5.625 g) of dry grated

Substitute: 1-1/2 Tbsp. (8.25 g) of fresh grated coconut

**Corn Syrup, Light**

Amount: 1 cup (237 ml)

Substitute: 1 cup (201 g) of sugar plus 1/4 cup (59 ml) of
the liquid already used in the recipe.

OR 1 cup honey (237 ml)

OR 1 cup agave nectar (237 ml)

OR 1 cup dark corn syrup (237 ml)

OR 1 cup liquid glucose (237 ml)

OR 1 cup treacle (237 ml)

**Corn Syrup, Dark**

¾ cup (178 ml) light corn syrup + ¼ cup (59 ml) light
molasses

**Cream, Whipping**

Amount: 1 cup, unwhipped (237 ml)

Substitute: If you wish to use a commercial pre-whipped
whipped cream or whipped cream substitute rather than
whip your own cream, use the guideline that 1 cup (237
ml) UNWHIPPED whipping cream expands to 2 cups when
WHIPPED. For example, if your recipe called for 1 cup of
cream to make whipped cream, you could substitute 2 cups
(474 ml) of an already whipped product.

**Cream**

Amount: 1 cup (237 ml)

Substitute: 1 cup (237 ml) Coconut cream

### Crème Fraîche

Amount: 1 cup (237 ml)

Substitute: 1 cup (237 ml) sour cream

OR 1 cup (237 ml) cream cheese

OR 1 cup (237 ml) mascarpone cheese

OR 1 cup (237 ml) whipping cream plus 1 Tbsp. (15 ml) buttermilk or yogurt

OR ½ cup (119 ml) whipping cream plus ½ cup (119 ml) sour cream

### Cream of Tartar

Amount: ½ tsp. (2.5 g)

Substitute: ½ tsp. (2.5 ml) white vinegar or lemon juice.

### Honey

Amount: 1 cup (237 ml)

Substitute: 1-1/4 cups sugar plus 1/4 cup liquid (use liquid called for in recipe) OR 1 cup corn syrup OR 1/2 - 2/3 cup agave syrup

### Lemon Zest (fresh grated lemon peel)

Amount: 1 tsp. (5 ml/5 g)

Substitute: 1/2 tsp. (2.5 ml/2 g) lemon extract

**Marshmallow Crème**
> Amount: 1 cup  (237 ml)
> Substitute: 16 large marshmallows
> OR 160 mini marshmallows plus 2 tsp. (10 ml) of light corn
>     syrup. Melt in a double boiler and stir until smooth

**Marshmallows, miniature**
> Amount: 1 cup  (237 ml)
> Substitute: 10 large marshmallows

**Mayonnaise**
> Amount: 1 cup (237 ml)
> Substitute:
> - 1 cup (237 ml) sour cream
> - 1 cup (237 ml) yogurt
> - 1 cup (237 ml) cottage cheese pureed in a blender
> - Or use any of the above for part of the mayonnaise

**Milk, Buttermilk**
> Amount: 1 cup (237 ml)
> Substitute: 1 cup minus 1 Tbsp. (15 ml) milk plus 1 Tbsp.
>     (15 ml) lemon or lime juice or white vinegar. Let sit 5
>     minutes and stir.
> OR powdered milk plus water to make the milk plus 1 Tbsp.
>     (15 ml) lemon or lime juice or white vinegar. Let sit 5
>     minutes and stir.
> OR ½ cup (119 ml) plain yogurt plus ½ cup (119 ml) milk
> OR ½ cup (119 ml) plain soy yogurt plus ½ cup (119 ml)
>     milk

**Milk, Evaporated**

Amount: 1 cup (237 ml)

Substitute: 1 cup (237 ml) half & half

OR 1 cup (237 ml) light whipping cream

OR 1 cup (237 ml) heavy whipping cream

**Milk, Sweetened Condensed**

Amount: 1 cup (237 ml)

Substitute: ½ cup (119 ml) evaporated milk plus ½ cup (119 ml) water

OR 1 cup (237 ml) skim or low fat milk plus 2 teaspoons (10 ml) of melted butter or coconut oil

**Milk, Whole**

Amount: 1 cup (237 ml)

Substitute: 1 cup (237 ml) coconut milk

**Pumpkin Pie Spice**

Amount: 1 tsp. (1.87 g)

Substitute: 1/2 tsp. (2.6 g) cinnamon plus 1/4 ground tsp. (1.1 g) ginger plus 1/8 tsp. (0.66 g) ground allspice plus 1/8 tsp. (0.29 g) ground nutmeg

**Rosewater**

Amount: Varies by substitution

Substitute: 1 Tbsp. (15 ml) lemon juice = 1-½ tsp. (7.5 ml) rosewater.

OR 1 tsp. (5 ml) orange juice = 1 tsp. (5 ml) rosewater.

OR make your own rosewater: 2 pesticide-free rose petals

plus 2 cups water. Bring water to a boil. Snip the ends
of the petals and pour the water onto the petals. Cover
with plastic wrap and let sit for 1 hour. Strain through a
colander lined with cheesecloth or a coffee filter.

## Rum
Amount: any amount
Substitute: 1 part rum extract plus 3 parts water. For
example: for 1/4 cup (59 ml) rum, substitute 1 Tbsp. (15
ml) rum extract plus 3 Tbsp. (45 ml) water

## Sugar, Confectioner's or Powdered
Amount: 1 cup (115 g)
Substitute: 1 cup granulated sugar plus 1 Tbsp. (213.6 g)
blended in your stand mixer until powdery
OR 2 parts Nonfat dry milk powder plus 2 parts cornstarch
plus 1 part sugar or the equivalent sugar replacement, mix
until well blended

**Sugar**, Regular Table – See Sugar Substitution Chart on page 112

# Flour & Flour Substitutes

**Weight, Measurement and Nutrition Equivalents**

(**King Arthur®** Brand noted with ^) (**Bob's Red Mill®** Brand noted with *)

| | Metric Weight | U.S. Ounces | U.S. Volume | Protein/ Serving | Fiber/ Serving | Carbs/ Serving | Calories/ Serving |
|---|---|---|---|---|---|---|---|
| 10 Grain Flour * | 120 g | 4.23 | 1 cup | 20 g | 8 g | 104 | 560 |
| All-Purpose Flour, Unbleached ^ | 120 g | 4.23 | 1 cup | 12 g | 4 g | 88 g | 440 |
| All-Purpose Gluten Free Flour * | 120 g | 4.23 | 1 cup | 12 g | 12 g | 88 g | 400 |
| Almond Flour, Blanched, non-toasted ^ | 75 g | 2.65 | 1 cup | 16 g | 11 g | 16 g | 480 |
| Almond Flour, toasted ^ | 80 g | 3.375 | 1 cup | 16 g | 11 g | 16 g | 480 |
| Amaranth Flour* | 120 g | 4.23 | 1 cup | 16 g | 12 g | 80 g | 440 |
| Arrowroot Powder * | 128 g | 4.52 | 1 cup | 0 | 4 g | 112 g | 440 |
| Barley Flour* | 120 g | 4.23 | 1 cup | 12 g | 20 g | 92 g | 424 |
| Malted Barley Flour * | 120 g | 4.23 | 1 cup | 16 g | 12 g | 80 g | 420 |
| Brown Rice Flour * | 160 g | 5.65 | 1 cup | 12 g | 4 g | 124 g | 560 |
| Buckwheat Flour * | 120 g | 4.23 | 1 cup | 16 g | 16 g | 44 g | 400 |
| Cake Flour, Spooned ^ | 104 g | 3.67 | 1 cup | 8 g | 2 g | 80 g | 360 |
| Chickpea Flour (Garbanzo Bean Flour) * | 120 g | 4.23 | 1 cup | 24 g | 20 g | 72 g | 440 |
| Coconut Flour * | 112 g | 3.95 | 1 cup | 16 g | 48 g | 80 g | 480 |
| Garbanzo Bean Flour * | 120 g | 4.23 | 1 cup | 24 g | 20 g | 72 g | 440 |

| | Metric Weight | U.S. Ounces | U.S. Volume | Protein/ Serving | Fiber/ Serving | Carbs/ Serving | Calories/ Serving |
|---|---|---|---|---|---|---|---|
| Gluten Free Garbanzo Fava Flour * | 120 g | 4.23 | 1 cup | 24 g | 24 g | 72 g | 440 |
| Gluten Free All Purpose Baking Flour * | 120 g | 3.23 | 1 cup | 12 g | 12 g | 88 g | 400 |
| Hazelnut Flour ^ | 104 g | 3.67 | 1 cup | 8 g | 4 g | 16 g | 640 |
| Kamut Flour * | 120 g | 4.23 | 1 cup | 12 g | 12 g | 84 g | 376 |
| Oat Flour * | 120 g | 4.23 | 1 cup | 21 g | 12 g | 78 g | 480 |
| Pastry Flour, White, Unbleached ^ | 104 g | 3.67 | 1 cup | 8 g | 0 | 80 g | 360 |
| Pastry Flour, White * | 136 g | 4.8 | 1 cup | 12 g | 0 | 108 g | 492 |
| Pastry Flour, Whole Wheat (a.k.a Graham Flour) ^ | 90 g | 3.17 | 1 cup | 9 g | 9 g | 66 g | 300 |
| Pastry Flour, Whole Wheat * | 120 g | 4.23 | 1 cup | 12 g | 16 g | 92 g | 440 |
| Potato Flour * | 181 g | 6.39 | 1 cup | 16 g | 11 g | 108 g | 640 |
| Quinoa Flour * | 112 g | 3.95 | 1 cup | 16 g | 8 g | 72 g | 440 |
| Sorghum Flour, Gluten Free * | 136 g | 4.8 | 1 cup | 16 g | 12 g | 100 g | 480 |
| Soy Flour * | 112 g | 3.95 | 1 cup | 40 g | 12 g | 32 g | 480 |
| Soy Flour, Defatted | 106 g | 3.75 | 1 cup | 50 g | 18 g | 41 g | 352 |
| Spelt Flour * | 120 g | 4.24 | 1 cup | 16 g | 8 g | 84 g | 400 |
| Tapioca Flour * | 120 g | 4.24 | 1 cup | 0 | 0 | 104 g | 400 |
| Teff Flour * | 120 g | 4.24 | 1 cup | 16 g | 16 g | 88 g | 452 |
| White Rice Flour * | 160 g | 5.64 | 1 cup | 8 g | 4 g | 128 g | 600 |
| White Bean Flour * | 128 g | 4.52 | 1 cup | 28 g | 32 g | 80 g | 440 |

| | Metric Weight | U.S. Ounces | U.S. Volume | Protein/ Serving | Fiber/ Serving | Carbs/ Serving | Calories/ Serving |
|---|---|---|---|---|---|---|---|
| Whole Wheat Flour, Traditional ^ | 120 g | 4.24 | 1 cup | 16 g | 16 g | 84 g | 440 |
| Whole Wheat Flour, White ^ | 120 g | 4.24 | 1 cup | 16 g | 12 g | 72 g | 400 |
| Whole Wheat Pastry Flour * | 120 g | 4.23 | 1 cup | 12 g | 16 g | 92 g | 440 |
| Xanthan Gum * | 144 g | 5.08 | 1 cup | 0 | 112 g | 112 g | 480 |

# Appendix B: Substitutions

*Appendix C*

# Cupcake Baking Terminology

**Agar (also known as Agar Agar):** A thickening agent made from a variety of different kinds of algae or seaweed. Agar is a gelatin-like substance when hydrated; firmer and stronger than gelatin.

**Air Cells/Air Bubbles:** The millions of tiny air pockets trapped inside the structure of starch and protein that form during the mixing and baking process. Mixing, heat and leavening are important in the formation of air cells.

**Albumen:** The white part of an egg, which is actually clear when the egg is in its raw form.

**Alkalized Cocoa Powder:** (also known as Dutch-process cocoa) Classic regular cocoa is acid based and bitter. When cocoa is treated with alkali, it goes from acid to alkaline, from light red-brown to dark red-brown, and mild to strong in flavor. Dutch-processed cocoas, which are alkalized, dissolve better in water.

**All-Purpose Flour:** Wheat flour that is milled from hard wheat or a blend of soft and hard wheat. Used in homes for some yeast breads, quick breads, cakes, cookies, pastries and noodles. All-purpose flour may be bleached or unbleached. Both may be enriched with four vitamins (niacin, riboflavin, folic acid, and thiamin) and iron. All-purpose flour may be used in a wide variety of home baked goods, such as cookies, quick breads, and some yeast breads.

**Allspice:** A single spice, rather than a combination of all spices, which is reminiscent of nutmeg, cloves, juniper berries, pepper, and cinnamon mixture. Allspice is made from the fruit of an evergreen tree found in the Western Hemisphere.

**Almond:** The kernel of the fruit of the almond tree. There are two types of almonds: sweet and bitter. Sweet almonds are used in cooking and can be eaten raw (either blanched without skins or with skins). Bitter almonds are usually distilled into an essence or extract which is used in baking. The sale of bitter almonds is illegal in the U.S.

**Almond Flour:** A non-gluten flour ground from the blanched kernels of the almond. Almond flour is one of the best non-gluten flour substitutes in baking to add nutrition for those without nut or tree nut allergies.

**Almond Paste:** A mixture of ground almonds, sugar and glucose used in baking recipes. Often used as a pastry filling.

**Amaranth Flour:** Milled from amaranth seeds, this flour combines well with other flours for smooth-textured quick breads. It has an assertive flavor and especially complements savory breads or pastries. Its lack of gluten means it must be combined with wheat flour in yeast breads.

**Amaretto:** A flavored liqueur made from apricot pits.

**Arrowroot:** A white, powdery starch ground finer than flour. It is used for thickening and is sometimes preferable to cornstarch because it does not turn cloudy. Arrowroot derives its name from Central American Indians who used it to heal arrow wounds. It is extracted from the tuberous rhizomes of the 6-foot perennial arrowroot plant.

**Aspartame:** Sold under the trade name Nutrasweet, this artificial sweetener is 180 times sweeter than sucrose. This sweetener is not recommended for baking.

**Bake:** To apply dry heat of a certain temperature to cook a cupcake recipe's ingredients in an oven. Oven should be pre-heated to the correct temperature prior to placing cupcakes in it.

**Baking Chocolate:** This unsweetened chocolate is also known as bitter chocolate. Baking chocolate has no added ingredients.

**Baking Powder:** A leavening agent made from a combination of baking soda, an acid (such as cream of tartar) and a moisture absorber (such as cornstarch). When baking powder is mixed with moist ingredients, carbon dioxide bubbles are released, causing batter to rise.

**Batter:** A pourable mixture of flour, liquid, leavening, flavoring and other ingredients.

**Beat:** The act of mixing ingredients with a circular motion quickly. Instruments used to beat include a hand mixer, stand mixer, food processor, wooden spoon and whisk.

**Blanch:** A method to partially cook and then suddenly stop the cooking process by plunging food into boiling water and then cold water.

**Boil:** The process of heating a liquid to the point where bubbles repeatedly rise to and break on the surface of the liquid.

**Bolted:** Flour that has been sifted through a screen or a fine sieve.

**Caramelize:** The process of melting and browning sugar over heat.

**Chop:** The act of cutting something into smaller pieces. The size of the pieces can range according to the recipe. "Finely" chop means to cut into very small pieces. "Coarsely" chop means larger pieces.

**Coats Spoon:** An indication of the state of a mixture when a metal spoon is dipped into a cooked mixture and drained, and an even film still covers the spoon.

**Cocoa Powder:** Chocolate powder that is a product of removing ¾ of the cocoa butter from chocolate liquor. Natural and Dutch processed unsweetened cocoa powder are two different types. Natural cocoa powder is acid based and tastes bitter, while the Dutch processed type is alkalized, dissolves easily in water and has a mild flavor. You cannot substitute one for the other in recipes without adding or subtracting acid based ingredients in the rest of the recipe. Dutch processed cocoa powder is used with acid containing baking soda.

**Coconut Oil:** A natural saturated fat vegetable oil from coconuts to which many have attributed a wide range of health benefits. Coconut oil is solid at 76°F, 23°C and liquid at 77°F, 24°C.

**Combine:** The process of mixing together two or more ingredients in a recipe.

**Cool:** The process of bringing a recipe to the recommended temperature after baking or cooking. Most often referring to room temperature unless otherwise stated.

**Cream:** The act of beating a mixture until is thoroughly mixed and fluffy.

**Cut In:** The process of using a pastry blender, long kitchen scissors, or two knives or forks to disperse solid butter or shortening among the dry ingredients of a recipe.

**Dash:** The measurement of any ingredient that is less than 1/8 tsp. (.6 ml). This is often a term used as a non-scientific measurement used liberally by experienced cooks.

**Dollop:** A heaping Tbsp. (or soup spoon)

**Dot:** The act of putting tiny dabs of frosting from the tip of a pastry tip onto the surface of baked goods.

**Drizzle:** The act of dripping icing from a spoon, a pastry bag or a fork.

**Dust:** The act of lightly sprinkling a dry ingredient like powdered sugar, flour, cinnamon or cocoa powder.

**Emulsifier:** Ingredients that have a dual attraction to water and oil that combine these two materials in blended solutions.

**Fold In:** The process of combining a heavy mixture with a lighter more delicate mixture such as meringue or whipped cream, slowly and gently, to preserve the air in the mixture.

**Gill:** A traditional British imperial unit of volume for liquid measurement, particularly alcohol from the UK. In the UK, 1 gill is equal to ¼ of a pint, 5 fluid ounces. In the U.S., 1 gill is equal to ½ cup or 4 fluid ounces. In Northern UK a gill is also known as a noggin. In southern UK the term large noggin is used and is equivalent to 2 gills.

**Glaze:** The process of coating with a thin liquid icing, jelly or preserves.

**Grate:** Shredding food with a food processor or any number of hand-held graters.

**Grease:** The act of rubbing shortening or other fat in a thin layer onto a cooking or baking surface to prevent food from sticking.

**Grind:** The process of running food through a grinder to get smaller particles of that food.

**Hygroscopic:** Draws and holds onto water preserving moistness in the cupcake.

**Lukewarm:** 105°F, 40°C. A temperature that feels warm, and is neither cold nor hot.

**Milk Chocolate:** A chocolate with sugar, cocoa butter, vanilla, lactose, and vegetable lecithin added.

**Mix:** The act of stirring two or more ingredients together until they are totally combined.

**Mix Until Moistened:** The act of stirring two or more ingredients together until they are combined and yet, the mixture is still lumpy.

**Pareve:** An ingredient that does not contain any dairy or meat-products.

**Peel:** To cut away the outside layer of a fruit or vegetable with a knife or peeler.

**Room Temperature:** 68°-72°F, 20°-22°C.

**Rind:** The outer layer or skin of a food. Thick cream, citrus fruit or cheese can have a rind.

**Rolling boil:** A "furious" boil. After water has been boiling for a longer time you can add ingredients into the pot and not affect the boil.

**Rounded teaspoon:** An ingredient mounded up on the tsp. instead of even with the edge. In milliliters it would fall between 5 ml and 7.5 ml. The grams would vary by the weight of the ingredient.

**Scald:** The act of heating a liquid or mixture right up to just below the boiling point.

**Score:** The act of cutting slits part way into the outer surface of a food with a knife.

**Softened:** The process of bringing fat, butter, shortening, margarine, mascarpone, cream cheese or ice cream to a temperature for easy mixing. Softened does not mean melted.

**Soft Peaks:** Mix egg whites or whipping cream by beating them with a whisk, stand or hand mixer to form soft, round peaks. Overbeating will break down the structure and cause the peaks to collapse.

**Stiff Peaks:** To beat egg whites to the stage where the mixture will hold stiff, pointed peaks when the beaters are removed.

**Stir:** To mix ingredients slowly in a circular motion with a spoon or whisk.

**Toss:** Using two spoons or forks gently lift and mix together.

**Types of Cupcakes:** Traditional cupcakes are classified much the same way cakes are. Cupcakes also have gone way beyond the traditional and can now be found in seemingly limitless varieties, mimicking the shape and size of a cupcake, though not in traditional cake tradition. Raw foods create raw cupcakes; cupcakes that by definition have no ingredients heated above 105°F, 40°C. There are also cupcakes that contain cookies and ice cream, breakfast ingredients, cheesecake and many more. Cupcake purists argue these are not really cupcakes. I don't take sides in that debate. If it's good food, I'll eat it. :)

**Whip:** The process of incorporating air into a mixture to lighten it or to increase the volume, by quickly mixing with a stand mixer, hand whisk or electric hand mixer.

**Zest:** The grated peel of a citrus fruit used to add flavor in recipes. Citrus fruits include grapefruit, orange, lemons and limes. The best way to create zest is to wash and dry the whole fruit and then use the tiniest holes of your food grater to gently rub the fruit to only collect the colored zest of the skin. You want to avoid the white part of the peel, it's bitter.

*Appendix D*

# Checklists

## Cupcake Baking Checklist

☐ Check to be sure Your Oven Thermometer is in the oven.

☐ Check the recipe for oven temperature.

☐ Preheat the oven.

☐ Take your refrigerated ingredients out.

☐ Gather the remainder of the ingredients needed for the cupcake, filling and frosting.

☐ Carefully read the whole recipe, check for any special instructions and any missing ingredients.

☐ Prepare and/or check the refrigerated ingredients to ensure they are warm (about room temperature 68°-70°F, 20°-22°C

☐ Prepare the batter, follow the recipe.

☐ Weigh/Measure the ingredients carefully.

☐ Fill the cupcake wells halfway to no more than 2/3 full; **do not** tap the tin on the counter to settle the batter.

☐ Check the oven thermometer to be sure the oven is at the exact temperature called for in the recipe before putting the cupcakes into the oven.

☐ Open the oven only as absolutely necessary (e.g., to turn the cupcake tin).

- ☐ Do not open the oven for any reason prior to the midpoint of the baking time.
- ☐ Check your cupcakes at the minimum baking time for doneness.
- ☐ Remove from oven when done (do not over bake).
- ☐ Remove from the tin after 3 minutes and place cupcakes on cooling racks to prevent over baking & problems with the cupcake papers.
- ☐ Let cool 1 hour on the cooling rack.
- ☐ Frost immediately when cool or wrap the cupcakes and freeze.
- ☐ Warm cupcakes to room temperature before frosting refrigerated or frozen cupcakes.

## Cupcake Ingredient Tips to Ensure Unforgettable Cupcakes

- ☐ Use the freshest ingredients you possibly can.
- ☐ Check your baking powder to ensure freshness.
- ☐ Crack you eggs into a separate bowl so you can keep eggshells and bad eggs out of your cupcake mix.
- ☐ Use cake flour (non self-rising) in preference to any other flour (adjust as necessary).
- ☐ Measure your flour first, and then sift it. This aerates the flour.
- ☐ Use real vanilla (not artificial or flavored) if the recipe calls for vanilla.
- ☐ Use unsalted butter. You want to control the amount of salt in the recipe yourself. Add a bit of salt to ramp up the flavor.
- ☐ Use superfine sugar instead of regular table sugar for a finer, lighter texture.

*Appendix E*

# Calculating the Calories and the Weight Watcher® Points for your Cupcakes

## How to Calculate Your Cupcakes' Calories

First, before you can calculate the calories, you will need to know or look up the number of calories for each ingredient in your recipe. Start with the cupcake itself, and then the filling and frosting. You can find the calorie count for each ingredient on the side panels of the ingredients in your kitchen, or you can visit a site such as www.GourmetSleuth.com and search their dictionary for your ingredients. Other excellent sites for ingredient nutrition research include www.NutritionData.com, www.KingArthurFlour.com, www.BobsRedMill.com, www.JoyofBaking.com and the USDA Ingredient Nutrition Database (website address is in the resources section). You can also Google the ingredient name along with the word "calories" or the words "nutritional information" and look for authoritative listings in the results.

A secret for finding an authority site to find your ingredient nutritional information is to limit results to either .edu or .gov sites or a specific authority site. Here are examples when searching for whole wheat flour:

1.  Limit your search to .edu (educational) or .gov (government) websites by typing the following in the search field:

    whole wheat flour nutritional data inurl:.edu inurl:.gov (make sure you do not put a space in between inurl: and the .edu and .gov

2.  Limit your search to a specific resource or website:

    a.  Whole wheat flour nutritional data inurl:kingarthurflour.com

    b.  Whole wheat flour nutritional data site:kingarthurflour.com

    You can also get more specific results by surrounding "whole wheat flour" in quotation marks. If you start off that way and don't get enough or any result you can always remove the quotation marks.

3.  Once you find sites you decide are favorites be sure to bookmark them so you can just go there first.

4.  You will find a ton of nutritional information in the tables in the Appendix at the back of this book.

Once you have the ingredient calories you may have to convert the calories to fit the amounts you have used in your recipe. Following is an example of how to convert calories for your ingredients to the amounts used in your recipes and how to calculate those calories per cupcake.

For example: If your cupcake recipe makes 24 regular cupcakes and has one cup of butter, 2 cups of superfine sugar, 3 cups of all-purpose flour, and 4 large eggs here is how to calculate the calories:

- 1 cup butter = 16 tablespoons at 100 calories per 1 tablespoon = 1600 calories
- 1 cup lowfat milk = 100 calories
- 2 cups superfine sugar = 1 teaspoon = 15 calories. 16 tablespoons per cup times 2 = 32 tablespoons times 3 teaspoons per tablespoon = 96 teaspoons times 15 calories = 1440 calories
- 3 cups all-purpose flour = 1 cup all-purpose flour = 440 calories times 3 cups = 1320 calories.
- 4 large eggs = 75 calories per large egg times 4 = 300 calories.

Total calories = 4,760 divided by the number of cupcakes, 24.

4,660/24 = 198.3 calories

Do the same for the filling and the frosting and add that to the calories per cupcake and voila!

Calculate grams of fat in your cupcakes:

Go through the same exercise above to determine the fat grams in each cupcake. Even some flours and milk have fat grams, so be sure you include the fat in all the ingredients.

Based on the recipe in the calories section above, the fat grams break down is as follows:

2 cups butter = 184 g
1 cup lowfat milk = 3 g
4 large eggs = 5 g per large egg times 4 eggs = 20 g
All-purpose flour = 0 g
Superfine sugar = 0 g

Total fat grams = 207 g

207 g/24 cupcakes = 8.625 or approximately 9 g of fat per cupcake.

Calculate Grams of Dietary Fiber for Your Cupcakes:

1 cup butter = 0 g
1 cup lowfat milk = 0 g
2 cups superfine sugar = 0 g
3 cups all-purpose flour = 3 grams per cup times 3 cups = 9 g
4 large eggs = 0 g
9 g/24 cupcakes = .375 g

How to Calculate the Points for Your Cupcakes:

Ever heard of a little eating program called Weight Watchers®? They use a point system to help guide you to fit any food into your day. Cupcakes make way. That's right, you can calculate your own cupcakes' points.

Here is the formula:
Points = (Calories/50) + (Fat Grams/12) − (min {Dietary Fiber, 4}/5)

The dietary fiber cannot exceed 4. If the cupcake has 5 grams of dietary fiber you can only use 4 in the formula. If the cupcake has 2 grams, then you use 2.

Here is an example using the recipe above (not including if you frost it):

Weight Watcher Points = (198/50) + (9/12) − (.375/5) = 3.96 + .75 - .075

= 4.425 or 5 points (points are rounded to the nearest whole point)

*Appendix F*

# Readings and Resources

## Books

Amendola, Joseph and Nicole Rees. *Understanding Baking.* Hoboken, New Jersey: John Wiley & Sons, Inc., 2003.

Amsterdam, Elana. *The Gluten-Free Almond Flour Cookbook.* Berkley, CA: Celestial Arts, 2009.

Barkie, Karen E. *Fancy, Sweet, & SugarFree.* New York: St. Martin's Press, 1985.

Beranbaum, Rose Levy. *The Cake Bible.* New York: William Morrow and Company, 1988.

Bloom, Carole. *The Essential Baker.* Hoboken, New Jersey: John Wiley & Sons, Inc., 2007.

Bryn, Anne. *The Cake Mix Doctor.* New York: Workman Publishing, 1999.

Catalano, Ania. *Baking with Agave Nectar.* Berkley, CA: Celestial Arts, 2008.

Child, Julia. *Baking with Julia Child.* New York: A La Carte Communications, Inc., 1996.

Corriher, Shirley O. *BakeWise.* New York: Scribner, 2008.

Culinary Institute of America. *Baking and Pastry.* Hoboken, New Jersey: John Wiley & Sons, Inc., 2004.

Culinary Institute of America, Richard J. Coppedge Jr., and Cathy Charles. *Gluten-Free Baking.* Avon, Massachusetts: Adams Media, 2008.

Darling, Jennifer. *Better Homes and Gardens New Cook Book.* Des Moines: Better Homes and Gardens, 2003.

Gisslen, Wayne. *Professional Cooking, 6th ed.* Hoboken, New Jersey: John Wiley & Sons, Inc., 2007.

Goldman, Marcy. *A Passion for Baking.* Birmingham, AL: Oxmoor House, Inc., 2007.

Hansen, Kaye and Liv. *Little Cakes from the Whimsical Bakehouse.* New York: Clarkston Potter/Publishers, 2008.

Keogh, Kelly E. *Sugar-Free, Gluten-Free Baking and Desserts.* Berkeley, CA: Ulysses Press, 2009.

Klivans, Elinor. *Cupcakes!* San Francisco, 2005.

King Arthur Flour Company, Inc. *The King Arthur Flour Baker's Companion.* Woodstock, Vermont: The Countryman Press, 2003.

Lewis, Matt and Renato Poliafito. *Baked: New Frontiers in Baking.* New York: Stewart, Tabori & Chang, 2008.

Malgieri, Nick. *How to Bake.* New York: Harper Collins, 1995.

Moskowitz, Isa Chandra and Terry Hope Romero. *Vegan Cupcakes Take Over the World.* New York: Marlowe & Company, 2006.

Niall, Mani. *Sweet!* Philadelphia, PA: Da Capo Press, 2008.

Ong, Pichet. *The Sweet Spot.* New York: HarperCollins, 2007.

Patent, Greg. *Baking in America.* New York: Houghton Mifflin Company, 2002.

Purdy, Susan G. *The Perfect Cake.* New York: Broadway Books, 2002.

Rinsky, Glen and Laura Halpin. *The Pastry Chef's Companion.* Hoboken, New Jersey: John Wiley & Sons, Inc., 2009.

Saulsbury, Camilla V. *Enlightened Cakes.* Nashville, TN: Cumberland House Publishing, Inc., 2008.

Stewart, Martha. *Cupcakes.* New York: Clarkson Potter/Publishing, 2009.

Sur La Table with Mushet, Cindy. *The Art & Soul of Baking*. Kansas City, KA: Andrews McMeel Publishing, LLC, 2008.

Tack, Karen & Alan Richardson. *Hello, Cupcake!* New York: Houghton Mifflin Company, 2008.

Yard, Sherry. *The Secrets of Baking*. New York: Houghton Mifflin Company, 2003.

Yockelson, Lisa. *Baking by Flavor*. New York: John Wiley & Sons, Inc. 2002.

## Articles

"43 Cake Baking Tips." *TipNut*. TipNut, n.d. Web. 2 June 2009.

"About Eggs: How to Crack and Separate." *Aki's Kitchen*. Aki's Kitchen, n.d. Web. 1 June 2009.

"Adding Mix-ins to Batter." Wilton. Wilton Industries, n.d. Web. 31 May 2009.

"All About Wheat, Fiber, Grain, Whole Grains, Whole Wheat, Carbohydrates, and More." *The Wheat Foods Council*. The Wheat Foods Council, n.d. Web. 15 Dec 2009.

Archuleta, Martha. "High Altitude Cooking, Guide E-215." *College of Agriculture and Home Economics*. New Mexico State University, Mar 2005. Web. 15 Dec 2009.

"Artisan Cupcakes—London—A Not So Guilty Pleasure." *The Organic Cupcake Company*. The Organic Cupcake Company, n.d. Web. 31 May 2009.

"Baking Pans." *Baking911*. Baking911, n.d. Web. 1 June 2009.

"Baking Soda vs. Powder." *GardenWeb*. iVillage, n.d. Web. 2 June 2009.

"Basic Cupcake Recipes." *Cupcake Ideas Now*. Belly Full Media, n.d.

Web. 1 June 2009.

Baughman, Mary. "Approaches to Insect Problems." *Harry Ransom Center*. The University of Texas at Austin, 20 Dec 2001. Web. 6 Dec 2009.

"Beat Whole Eggs." *Baking911*. Baking911, n.d. Web. 1 June 2009.

Berman, Amy. "How to Make the Perfect Birthday Cake." *Celebrations*. Celebrations, n.d. Web. 1 June 2009.

Brandt, Laura. "Emulsifiers in Baked Goods." *Food Product Design*. Virgo Publishing, LLC, 1 Feb 1996. Web. 15 Dec 2009.

Byrn, Anne. "What's in a Cake Mix?" *iVillage Food*. iVillage, Inc., 17 Nov 2009. Web. 15 Dec 2009.

"Buttery Spreads." *ButterySpreads.org*. National Association of Margarine Manufacturers, n.d. Web. 15 Dec 2009.

"Cake Baking Techniques." *Aki's Kitchen*. Aki's Kitchen, n.d. Web. 1 June 2009.

"Cake Glossary." *The Nibble*. Lifestyle Direct, n.d. Web. 2 June 2009.

"Cake Ingredients." *Baking 911*. Baking 911, n.d. Web. 15 Dec 2009.

"Cake Making Tips." *101 Lifestyle*. 101 Lifestyle, n.d. Web. 1 June 2009.

"Cake Mixes." *Baking911*. Baking911, n.d. Web. 2 June 2009.

Castella, Krystina. "Crazy About Cupcakes." *Crazy About Cupcakes*. Crazy About Cupcakes, n.d. Web. 1 June 2009.

—. "For Great Cakes, Get the Ratios Right." *Fine Cooking*. Taunton Press, Inc., n.d. Web. 2 Jan 2010.

"Cookie Hints." *The Baking Pan*. The Baking Pan, n.d. Web. 1 June 2009.

"Cupcakes." *Bon Appetite*. Bon Appetite, n.d. Web. 1 June 2009.

"Cupcake Batter Amounts." *Wilton*. Wilton Industries, n.d. Web. 31 May 2009.

Durand, Faith. "Why From-Scratch Cakes are Healthier Than Box Mix Cakes." *The Kitchen*. Apartment Therapy, 27 Feb. 2008. Web. 1 June 2009.

"Easy Recipes, Healthy Eating Ideas and Chef Recipe Videos." *Food Network*. Television Food Network, n.d. Web. 6 Dec 2009.

"Eggs." *Baking911*. Baking911, n.d. Web. 1 June 2009.

"Filling Cups with Batter." *Wilton*. Wilton Industries, n.d. Web. 31 May 2009.

Fogt, Robert. "Common Weight and Mass Conversions." *Online Conversion*. Online Conversion, n.d. Web. 6 Dec 2009.

"For the Love of Cupcakes." *National Public Radio*. National Public Radio, 17 October 2007. Web. 2 June 2009.

"Frequently Asked Questions." *Sweet Debbie's Organic Cupcakes*. Sweet Debbie's Organic Cupcakes, n.d. Web. 31 May 2009.

"Frequently Asked Questions." *White Lily*. The J.M. Smucker Company, n.d. Web. 15 Dec 2009.

Gail. "Angel Food Cupcakes." *Allrecipes*. Allrecipes, n.d. Web. 31 May 2009.

"Gill (Measurement)." *Encyclopedia Britannica Online*. Encyclopedia Britannica, n.d. Web. 2 Jan 2010.

Hackett, Jolinda. "What Can I Use to Substitute for Eggs in a Recipe?" *About.com Guide*. The New York Times Company, n.d. Web. 2 Jan 2010.

Henneman, Alice. "Ingredient Substitutions." *University of Nebraska-Lincoln*. University of Nebraska-Lincoln, n.d. Web. 15 Dec 2009.

"How Not to Ship a Cupcake: The Results." *Cake Spy*. Cake Spy, 20 Dec 2007. Web. 15 Dec 2009.

"How to Make a Delicious, Healthy Cake from Scratch." *Giant Eagle*. Giant Eagle, n.d. Web. 1 June 2009.

"How to Make a Perfect Cake." *Recipe Finder.* NineMSN, n.d. Web. 1 June 2009.

"How to Prepare a Cake Pan." *Baking911.* Baking911, n.d. Web. 1 June 2009.

"How to Replace Eggs in Cooking." *EHow.* EHow, n.d. Web. 2 June 2009.

"Human Powered Search." *Mahalo.* Mahalo.com Incorporated, n.d. Web. 15 Dec 2009.

"Ice Cream Cone Cakes Recipe." *Betty Crocker.* General Mills, n.d. Web. 6 Dec 2009.

"Incredible Edible Egg." *IncredibleEgg.org.* American Egg Board, 2009. Web. 2 Jan 2010.

"Inspiration for Every Celebration." *Wilton.* Wilton Industries, n.d. Web. 6 Dec 2009.

Irvine, Don. "Let Them Eat Cupcakes." *Accuracy in Academia.* Accuracy in Academia, 2006. Web. 2 June 2009.

Jacquin, Amy. "Kitchen Aid Silicone Bakeware." *KFVS Heartland News.* Raycom Media, n.d. Web. 6 Dec 2009.

Jaworski, Stephanie and Rick. "Butter or Shortened Cakes Recipe." *Joy of Baking.com.* Joy of Baking.com, n.d. Web. 2 Jan 2010.

—. "Cocoa Powder." *Joy of Baking.com.* Joy of Baking.com, n.d. Web. 2 Jan 2010.

—. "Muffin Recipes." *Joy of Baking.com.* Joy of Baking.com, 2010. Web. 2 Jan 2010.

—. "Sugars." *Joy of Baking.com.* Joy of Baking.com, n.d. Web. 2 June 2009.

Jyotsna, R, Prabhasankar, D, Indrani, G, and Venkateswara, Rao. "Improvement of Rheological and Baking Properties of Cake Batters with Emulsifier Gels." *Journal of Food Science* 69.1 (2008):

SNQ16-SNQ19. Web. 15 Dec 2009.

Karen. "Sticky Pecan Upside-Down Cupcakes." *Recipezaar.* Scripps Networks, 5 Sept. 2009. Web. 6 Dec 2009.

Kittencal. "Almost Cake Mix Vanilla Cupcakes." *Recipezaar.* Scripps Networks, n.d. Web. 31 May 2009.

Kooyman, Milt. "Weather Conversion Calculators." Weather Conversion Calculators, n.d. Web. 2 Jan 2010.

Lisa. "Sunshine S'more Cupcakes." *Allrecipes.* Allrecipes, n.d. Web. 31 May 2009.

Love, Diana. "Annapolis Cupcake Shop Full of Sweet Creations." *Hometown Annapolis.* Capital Gazette Communications, 13 May 2009. Web. 31 May 2009.

Margen, Sheldon and Dale Ogar. "Eggs: Whites vs. Yolks." *Third Age.* Third Age, 27 August 2007. Web. 1 June 2009.

Martin, Andrew. "The School Cafeteria, On a Diet." *The New York Times.* New York Times Company, 5 September 2007. Web. 2 June 2009.

Mayers, A. "History of the Cupcake." *All About Cupcakes.* All About Cupcakes, n.d. Web. 31 May 2009.

"Muffin Tins." *Cook's Illustrated.* America's Test Kitchen, 2005. Web. 1 June 2009.

Olson, Elizabeth. "The Latest Entrepreneurial Fantasy Is Selling Cupcakes." *The New York Times.* The New York Times Company, 25 Nov 2009. Web. 2 Jan 2010.

"Online Shopping for Apparel, Computers, Books, DVDs and More." *Amazon.com.* Amazon.com, Inc., n.d. Web. 6 Dec 2009.

Parisi, Grace. "Angel Food Cupcakes with Raspberry Swirl Recipe." *Food & Wine.* American Express Publishing, n.d. Web. 6 Dec 2009.

"Preparing the Batter." *Wilton.* Wilton Industries, n.d. Web. 31 May

2009.

"Preparing the Pan." *Wilton*. Wilton Industries, n.d. Web.31 May 2009.

Qureshi, Huma. "The World's Largest Cupcake." *Word of Mouth Blog*. Guardian News and Media Limited, 17 July 2009. Web. 6 Dec 2009.

Robertson-Boyd, Laura. "Why Do Cupcake Papers Separate from the Cupcakes after Baking?" *BakingSOS Answers*. BakingSOS Answers, n.d. Web. 2 Jan 2010.

Salima, Candace. "Recipe: Mixes vs. Scratch." *Dream a Little Dream Blog*. Dream a Little Dream Blog, 23 Nov. 2008. Web. 1 June 2009.

Schulte, Brigid. "Once Just a Sweet Treat, The Cupcake Becomes a Cause." *The Washington Post*. The Washington Post, 11 December 2006. Web. 31 May 2009.

Shioya, Tara. "What is the difference between wet and dry measuring cups?" *Chow.com*. CBS Interactive, 18 Oct. 2007. Web. 31 May 2009.

"Silicone Cookwear." *Green Living Tips*. Green Living Tips, n.d. Web. 1 June 2009.

Smith, S.E. "What is a Cake Tester?" *Wise Geek*. Conjecture Corporation, n.d. Web. 1 June 2009.

Stradley, Linda. "Egg White Meringue—How To Make Perfect Meringue." *What's Cooking America*. What's Cooking America, n.d. Web. 2 Jan 2010.

"Substitutions." *Dartmouth*. Dartmouth College, n.d. Web. 15 Dec 2009.

"The Creaming Method." *Squidoo*. Squidoo, n.d. Web. 2 June 2009.

"Types of Bakeware." *Recipe Tips*. Recipe Tips, n.d. Web. 1 June 2009.

Watkins, Diana. "The Perfect Cake." *Easy Southern Cooking*. Easy

Southern Cooking, n.d. Web. 1 June 2009.

"What is Creaming?" *Baking911*. Baking911, n.d. Web. 2 June 2009.

"What Recipes May Not Tell You." *Science of Cooking*. Exploratorium, n.d. Web. 2 Jan 2010.

"Why you need a cooling rack." *Baking Bites*. Baking Bites, n.d. Web. 1 June 2009.

Woodall, Diana. "Conversion Calculators." Diana's Desserts, n.d. Web. 15 Dec 2009.

"Your Online Source of Gluten-Free Food for your Celiac Disease Diet." *GlutenFree.com*. GlutenFree.com, n.d. Web. 15 Dec 2009.

# Online Tools

**USDA Online Database to look up Nutrient Information for Your Ingredients:**

> http://www.nal.usda.gov/fnic/foodcomp/search/

**Online Calculator to Increase or Decrease the Number of Cupcakes for Your Recipes:**

> www.fruitfromwashington.com/Recipes/scale/recipeconversions.php

**Online Calculator to Determine the Nutritional Data for Your Cupcake Recipes (Per Serving):**

> www.nutritiondata.com
>
> Recipes.sparkpeople.com/recipe-calculator.asp
>
> Caloriecount.about.com/cc/recipe_analysis.php
>
> www.gourmetsleuth.com

**Food Dictionary:** www.epicurious.com/tools/fooddictionary

**Almonds:** www.almondboard.com and www.clanaspantry.com

**Egg Nutritional Information:**

> www.incredibleegg.org

**Flours:** www.kingarthurflour.com

**Alternative Flours:** www.bobsredmill.com

**Great Cupcake Blogs**

**The Cupcake Bakeshop**

> By Cheryl Pocco, Chemical Engineer by day, cupcake baker by

night. You'll find lots of great cupcake recipes on Cheryl's blog
http://cupcakeblog.com

**Bakerella**

By the Cake Pop Queen of the World. Sweet recipes and amazing cupcake decorating ideas.
http://www.bakerella.com/

**Cupcakes Take the Cake**

By Rachael "Cupcake by Day, Dish by Night" Kramer Bussel, Nichelle Stephens and Stacie Joy
http://cupcakestakethecake.blogspot.com/

**JavaCupcake** – Fun, fresh cupcake blog written by Army Wife, Betsy. She shares her obsession with cupcakes and her recipes.
http://javacupcake.blogspot.com/

**CupcakeDecoratingU.com** (Home of the Cupcake Inspiration Index) Compiled by the Cupcake Chef
An ever-growing resource for cupcake decorating ideas.
www.CupcakeDecoratingU.com

**Other Sweet Blogs**

**The Pioneer Woman** – The adventures of Ree Drummond, her Marlboro Man and good food.
http://thepioneerwoman.com/

**Elana's Pantry** – Author of "The Gluten-Free Almond Cookbook." She turned me on to Almond Flour, which is a great healthy way to pack heart healthy, high protein and mineral nutrition into your cupcakes. Her book includes some wonderful cupcake recipes.
www.elanaspantry.com

. . . . . . . . . . . . . . . . . . . . . . . . . . . . . . . . . . . . . . . . . . . . . . . . . . . . . . . . . . . . .

**Wonderful Baking Catalogs**

CentralChef – www.CentralChef.com

**Interested in starting your own cupcake bakery or baking business?**

**Visit www.BakingBusinessU.com** to download a FREE baking business plan for a retail, home-based or mobile bakery business of your own. Includes full sample business plan and calculating spreadsheets to get you started today.

. . . . . . . . . . . . . . . . . . . . . . . . . . . . . . . . . . . . . . . . . . . . . . . . . . . . . . . . . . . . .

330

## Symbols

7-Minute Frosting  188
7-UP  238

## A

acidity  91
adjustment  96, 97, 238, 282
  for Altitude  282
  for Humidity  281
  type of leavening  51, 92
agar  187
Agar  126, 128, 129
agave  126, 187, 189, 209, 243, 244,
    248, 254
air bubbles  233, 238, 255
allergies  46, 58, 300
all-purpose flour  79, 80, 81
almond extract  57
almond flour  294
almond milk  102
aluminum pans  249, 250
amaranth Flour  300
angel food  241, 248, 256
Angel food  258
anise  259
apple butter  102
apple pie spice  259
apple Pie Spice  285
apples  98, 102, 108, 120, 202, 244
applesauce  102, 244
arrowroot  85, 248, 285, 294, 300
articles on cupcakes  319
aspartame  300

## B

bakeries  46, 47, 197, 221, 245
baker's chocolate  181
baking
  chemical reactions  249
  convection oven  266
  temperature  282, 283, 301
baking cups  67, 158, 230, 258
baking pans  64
baking powder  51, 52, 53
baking soda  34, 51, 52, 53
baking terminology  275
baking time  56, 65, 112, 157, 167,
    168, 169, 230, 232, 233, 237,
    240, 246, 257, 258
bananas  99, 102, 120
beating  144, 145, 146
Blended Melted Method  148
blogs  34, 327
blueberries  144
boiled frosting  180, 187, 188
bonding  38
books  317
box mixes  53, 54, 55, 57, 241, 259
bread-like texture  139, 142
browning  66, 67
brown rice flour  85, 86, 87
bubbles  51, 53
buckwheat flour  294
buttercream  175, 176, 177, 178,
    179, 180
buttermilk  195, 233, 263, 265, 267

## C

cake flour 55, 79, 80
cake mixes 34, 54, 56, 57, 89, 255
candied fruit 187
candy bars 246
candy stuffings 207
caramel filling (dulce de leche) 187, 189
caramelizing 127
cardamom 285
carob powder 288
carrots 102
carrying cases 217
Celsius to Fahrenheit conversion 280
charts
  butter volume and weight 101
  by ingredients and function 126
  egg size 231
  egg substitution 119
  fat substitution 98
  flour substitution 294
  frosting and icing 188
  sugar substitution 112
  volume measurement 278
checklists 307
chemical leaveners. *See* soda and baking powder
cherries 203, 208
chickpea flour 294
chiffon 176, 241, 248, 258
chocolate buttercream 181, 188
chocolate chips 40, 144, 215, 255, 287
chocolate frostings 48, 49, 181
cinnamon 235, 259

citrus peel 259
cloves 285, 300
cocoa powder 288, 299, 302, 303
coconut 99, 100, 102, 187, 215, 223, 241, 248, 252, 253, 302
coconut flour 86, 294
coconut oil 68, 96, 98, 99, 100, 102, 187, 252, 253, 265, 266, 267, 302
combination melted method 147, 148
commercial mixes 55
condensed milk 292
confectioner's sugar 106, 182, 185, 258, 293
convection oven 266
Cool Whip® 178, 236
corn syrup 180, 289, 290, 291
cracking eggs 63, 117
cream cheese 176, 178, 179
cream frosting 175, 178
creaminess 115, 176
creaming method 141, 144
cream of tartar 92, 126, 128, 286, 287, 288, 290
cream, sour 91, 178, 186, 187, 188, 195, 233, 290, 291
cream, whipped 178
Crisco® 68. *See also* shortening
Crocker, Betty 34
crumb 51, 80, 89, 91, 96, 97, 102, 115, 116, 145, 148, 153, 154
cups, baking 158
curdled mixtures 118, 145
curdling 132

## D

dairy-free 187, 188, 209
dates 39, 75, 98, 99, 102, 258
date sugar 265, 267
decorating 123, 161, 198, 201, 215, 254, 328
decorating bag 123, 161
decorator's buttercream 186, 189
diabetic substitutes 106, 109, 110
dietary fiber 314, 315
double-acting baking powder 92, 93, 286
dried egg whites 175, 186
dried fruit 129, 179, 187
dulce de leche 187, 189
Dutch processed cocoa 288, 302

## E

egg foam method 141, 146, 147, 148
egg-white frostings 179, 187
egg yolks 53, 89, 117, 119, 126, 127, 128, 146, 264, 267
emulsifiers 89, 115, 126, 303
espresso powder 259
evaporated milk 292

## F

fiber 79, 268, 294, 314, 315
figs 179, 187
flat frostings. *See* glazes
flavorings 55
flaxmeal 119
fluffy frosting 180, 188, 281
foil cups 67

folding 96, 97, 144, 145
fondant 40, 186, 189
food sensitivities 58
freezing 76, 213, 214
fresh fruit 128, 198, 237, 248, 258
fructose 106, 114
fruit juice 185
fruit preserves 187, 199
fruit puree 108, 244
fudge frosting 181, 188

## G

ganache 40, 176, 181, 182, 189, 254, 257, 258
garbanzo fava flour 295
garbanzo flour 294, 295
gifts 39, 41, 213, 217
ginger 292
glazes 185, 189
gluten 68, 78, 79, 80, 84, 85, 86, 87
glycemic index values 112
golden buttercream 177, 188, 248, 269
graham flour 295
grated citrus peel 259
gum paste 129

## H

hazelnut flour 295
high altitude baking 121, 241, 282
honey 91, 106, 107, 112, 126, 127, 187, 244, 254, 289, 290
Humidity 281
humidity adjustment 233, 281, 282

## I

ice cream cones  250, 251
ice cream scoop  123, 241
icings  177, 185, 189
Italian buttercream  177, 180, 188, 248, 271

## K

Kamut Flour  295
King Arthur® flour  294
kosher certification  109, 110

## L

lactose-free  187
Lady Baltimore cupcake  179
lard  100, 128. *See also* fat
lecithin  89, 99, 115, 119, 303
lemon and lime zest  57, 248, 290, 305
lemon juice  57, 93, 263, 265, 266, 271, 286, 287, 288, 290, 292
lowfat milk  313, 314

## M

Malted Barley Flour  294
maple syrup and sugar  107
margarine  95, 96, 98, 100, 304
marshmallows  123, 291
mascarpone  206, 270, 290, 304
mayonnaise  233, 291
melted method  147, 148
meringue frostings  179
metallic taste  155, 249
metric conversions  277
milk chocolate frosting  181

miniature candy bars  246
mix-ins  123, 255
moisteners  125, 126
molasses  91, 107, 113, 286, 289
molten chocolate  49, 257
muffin-like texture  143
muffin method  141, 142, 143
muffin pans  66, 249

## N

non-stick pans  229, 249, 254
non-stick spray  68, 69, 248
nutmeg  235, 285, 292, 300
nuts  85, 123, 179, 207, 258

## O

Oat Flour  295
olive oil  115, 252, 253
online tools  275
orange juice  292
organic ingredients  55, 57, 58
oven rack placement  168
oven temperature  63, 65, 107, 112, 121, 167, 168, 232, 240, 244, 254
oven thermostat  65
overbaking  169
overmixing  137, 138

## P

packaging  75, 220
pairing cupcake with frosting  176
Pam® cooking spray  68
pareve  303
party nut cups  221, 247, 250

pastry bags  198
pastry flour  77, 80, 82
pears  98, 99
pectin  129
potato flour  295
powdered fructose  106
powdered sugar  158, 177, 179
preserves  187, 199, 303
prunes  98, 99, 102
pumpkin  98, 99, 102, 108, 142, 176
pumpkin pie spice  292
PureVia™ sweetener  109, 110

### Q

quinoa  55, 77, 85, 86, 87

### R

raisins  179
rancidity  75, 77
Reb-A extract  108
Red Mill® flours  87, 115, 265, 294
reduced-calorie recipes  96
removing cupcakes from pan  157, 169
rewarding loyalty  42
rice milk  102
rosewater  292
royal icing  185, 186
rubbing in  145
rum  185, 293

### S

Salmonella  175
salt  73, 83, 98, 100, 117, 126, 138, 195, 270, 271
satin ganache  182, 189
sea level  121, 282, 283
self-filling cupcakes  201, 204, 206, 207
self-rising flour  77, 82, 83
semi-sweet chocolate  206, 253
seven-minute frosting  180
sherry  57
shipping containers  219
shortening  68, 69, 73, 95, 96
sifting  79, 145
sifting flour  79, 82
simple chocolate buttercream  181, 188
S'more cupcakes  55
soda pop  259. *See also* 7UP
sodium bicarbonate. *See* baking soda
sorghum flour  85, 86
soy flour  295
soy lecithin  89, 115
soy milk  265, 266
specialty frostings  186, 209
spelt  77, 295
spices  300
Splenda  107, 114
sponge cakes  116, 117, 146, 194, 256, 281, 283
sprinkles  123, 170, 215, 239, 242
statistics  25, 34, 47
Stevia  106, 107, 108, 109, 110
stir and spoon method  81

strengtheners 126
sucralose 107
sugar cones 251
Sun Crystals® 108, 109, 110, 113
superfine sugar 52, 144, 206, 232, 309, 313, 314
sweeteners 106, 126
swiss buttercream 177, 188
syrup 177, 180

**T**

table sugar 112, 144, 309
tapioca flour 85, 265, 295
tapioca starch 85
tartaric acid. *See* cream of tartar
teff 295
tenderizers 125, 126, 193
terminology 299
thermometer, candy 271
thermostat 65
thickeners 129
tins 34, 65, 66, 67, 68
tips 25, 45, 47, 198, 214, 236, 281, 309
tofu 119
tools, kitchen 62, 64
transporting cupcakes 213, 217
traveling with cupcakes 213, 221, 224
treacle 289
troubleshooting 229
truffle frosting 182, 189, 246
Truvia™ sweetener 109, 110
tunnels in cupcakes 238

**U**

unsweetened chocolate 287, 301

**V**

vanilla 34, 54, 55, 58
vegan 84, 96, 249, 253
vegetable shortening 176, 186, 249
volume conversion 115, 194, 277, 278
volume measurement 61, 62, 279

**W**

water
   as substitute for milk 291
   as substitute to milk 292
wax paper 214, 256
Weight Watcher® points 311, 315
whipped cream 175, 176, 178, 179
whipping
   cream 281, 289, 290, 292, 304
   eggs 96, 97, 146, 281
   frosting 182
whipping egg whites 146, 281
whisking method 146
white bean flour 296
white chocolate frosting 181
white truffle frosting 182
whole wheat flour 78, 79, 82
wrapping cupcakes 215

**X**

xanthan gum 86, 296
xylitol 106, 110, 111

## Y

yogurt
  as egg substitute  119
  as fat substitute  98, 99
  as milk substitute  291
  in frostings  187, 189, 248

## Z

Ziploc  161, 198, 203, 245
Zsweet  109, 110
zucchini  102

# About the Author

Isabella Anjuli is a mother of two beautiful daughters and is a really bad poet. That is why she wrote a book about cupcakes.

A military brat and restless spirit, Isabella was born at Fort Benning, Georgia to a U.S. Army Captain with the airborne division and was a military wife and mother in support of the U.S. Air Force. She has traveled to all 50 states in America and lived and baked cupcakes in the beautiful states of Georgia, Hawaii, Michigan, Illinois, Virginia, Colorado and Florida.

Isabella lived in Japan for a bit as a little girl where she fell in love with a little dog named Wetsu that began her lifelong love of animals. Shortly afterwards, she made another life altering discovery when she decided cupcakes were a much safer option than a cake after her mother accidentally set her own hair on fire when lighting the candles on Isabella's 5th birthday cake (Isabella's mom was fine and surprisingly still uses hairspray).

A graduate of the University of West Florida, Isabella's restless spirit met Texas and it was love. She discovered she is a diehard Texan at heart. Go Longhorns! She is currently searching for property in Texas to call home.

Isabella constantly experiments with new, healthier cupcake recipes. She is currently working on a follow up cupcake recipe book filled with her super secret cupcake recipes. You can sign up for all the taste bud mind altering scoops at http://cupcakeaffair.com/breakingnews.

# About the Publisher

Are you an expert at something? Have you written a book on the subject or would you like to become a recognized expert in your field with all the perks that come with it? Asher Drake Publishing puts tomorrow's experts in the spotlight today. Cash in on your expertise. For more information visit:

http://asherdrakepublishing.com/authors

LaVergne, TN USA
20 February 2011
217250LV00006B/32/P

9 780984 577408